COME, FOLLOW ME

*Come unto me, all ye that labour and are heavy laden,
and I will give you rest.*

Matthew 11:28 KJV

BY SHIRLEY AMENDT

DEDICATION

I dedicate these poems to my Savior and my Lord, Jesus Christ. I thank God for the poems, because He gave them to me. I now return them to God, and place them in His hands.

*I thank my husband, Joe, my son, Chuck, my daughter, Catherine, and my daughter-in-law, Jeni, for their constant help and encouragement. I thank my dear friend, Teresa, for her continuing advice and enthusiasm. My wonderful church family at Prairie Lakes Baptist has listened to my readings and supported me in my book writing efforts!
I love and thank each one of you!*

And last, but not least, I thank all my dear friends who believed in my abilities, and loved my story-poems!

TABLE OF CONTENTS

Still looking like a little girl, my Mary came to me,
She hugged me like a loving child; her smile was good to see!

*39 And Mary arose in those days, and went into the hill country with
haste, into a city of Juda;*
40 And entered into the house of Zacharias, and saluted Elisabeth.

Luke 1:39,40 KJV

HIS NAME IS JOHN

I was a barren woman for lo, these many years,
In our early days my husband came close to shedding tears.

His dream was for a baby boy, to carry on his name,
Month by month we waited, but our son never came.

He never looked for someone else, was proud I was his wife,
I can't deny the two of us, had a good and happy life.

Both of us descended from respected priestly lines,
Both of us loved the Lord with all our hearts and minds.

We knew that if the Lord was pleased, that we have no son,
We must not be bitter, or regret there wasn't one.

Zechariah loved to serve his time as temple priest,
This only happened once before, and he was very pleased.

He traveled to Jerusalem, and I remained at home,
It was a little lonely, but I enjoyed my time alone.

This time, in our later years, I wished he would not go,
I never said a word of this, and I'm sure he did not know.

I missed my husband sorely; I worried for his health.
I knew I needed Zechariah more than any wealth.

So I waited with impatience, through our time apart,
I stayed busy with the household, and hushed my anxious heart.

When his time was finished, and then he came back home,
I found him very changed from the man I'd always known.

This new Zechariah was dumb and could not speak,
He kept a humble countenance, prayerful and quite meek.

Whatever had befallen him, he had no way to tell,
I told myself this would pass, that he would soon be well.

He would not write his story down for curious friends to read,
And I never learned my letters, for it seemed there was no need.

Zechariah seemed distracted, thinking thoughts I could not guess,
Yet he seemed to want to please me--even more--not less!

We were close as we hadn't been, since we first were wed,
I wondered what befell him, but it was trapped inside his head.

I prayed that Zechariah would have his speech return,
I tried hard to read his lips, but I couldn't seem to learn.

Then suddenly I was ill, it came and seemed to stay!
It didn't stop--it just went on--ruining part of every day.

I slept too much--I couldn't eat--for no reason I could name,
Until I saw my neighbor's wife was feeling much the same.

I was amazed--I dared not hope, and still the feeling grew,
I looked into my husband's eyes, he smiled, and then I knew.

Though past the age to bear a child, it seemed as though I would,
Like Sarah and like Hannah, God was showing me I could!

I went into seclusion, this was a special private thing,
God was giving me a child--it was like a second spring!

It wasn't long till I could feel, the baby move and kick,
My appetite exploded, and I was no longer sick.

We would have a little son, I was sure that this was so!
A girl is held beneath your ribs; a boy is carried low.

I wished a friend would come to me, for company and cheer,
Zechariah couldn't speak, though I loved that he stayed near.

I longed for little Mary, who lived some ways from me,
My happy little cousin was the one I longed to see.

I did not think she would come, for her life was busy there.
And yet I kept a tiny hope that God would heed my prayer.

The sixth month came upon me, I grew heavy and quite tired,
It was then my little Mary, came just as I desired.

I saw her running up the path; she was calling out my name!
I could see she was a woman now, but still looked much the same.

The spirit of God came over me, very strong and sweet,
Such joy and wonder filled my heart that I almost had to weep!

"Blessed are you, among women," I cried, "and blessed this child you bear!
I am more glad than you can know, just to see you standing there!"

"Our God has given you a gift, that all the world will see!
And why does the mother of my Lord, come here to visit me?"

"I felt the babe within me move, as you were drawing near!
This child within leapt with joy when your voice fell on my ear!"

"For the woman who receives, a promise from the Lord,
Blessed is she who believes, that He fulfills His word."

Still looking like a little girl, my Mary came to me,
She hugged me like a loving child; her smile was good to see!

Mary spoke quite eagerly, and her words were like a song.
She said her days were wonder filled, to last her whole life long.

"My soul rejoices in my savior, and the Lord is magnified!
I am His humble servant. In Him I will abide.

All generations from now on, will see and call me blessed,
The Holy One has raised me up, and in His love I rest."

Such peace was glowing in her face, such love was in her eyes,
God had surely favored her; I never questioned why.

Mary told me she would stay until my baby came,
Every day was happy now, everything had changed.

Mary greeted Zechariah and she knew right away,
The secret he was keeping, the thing he could not say.

"You have seen an angel! Please nod if this is true!
I understand what's happened, for I have seen him too!"

Zechariah seemed at peace that Mary understood,
She was quick to read his lips, and I was glad she could!

With Mary's help, I could enjoy the waiting for our son,
I tried hard to ease her sickness, for her child had just begun.

Mary seemed very tired, and sometimes couldn't eat.
But I had just been through it all, so I let her sleep.

Morning rest was Mary's time, and mine was afternoon,
I grew awkward and impatient, but the babe was coming soon.

And when my time at last arrived, my Mary was still there!
Zechariah was kind and sweet, but I wanted Mary's care.

Labor started early when the day had just begun,
Mary answered when I called, for she had risen with the sun.

"I am feeling well today. I think my sick time's past."
Her words were sunlight to my soul, for the babe was coming fast.

I feared because I was so old, his birth might be my end,
I prayed that I was ready, for whatever God might send.

Labor wasn't easy, and I was racked with pain,
I told myself that for this child, I'd do it all again.

Zechariah's gentle eyes showed his pleasure and his care,
He and Mary prayed and helped, until the child was there.

In joy I saw our baby boy, I held him in my arms;
I prayed that we'd live long enough, to keep him safe from harm.

Friends and family gathered, to share our joyful state,
A baby born at our age, was a cause to celebrate!

Our cousin, Jeremiah, said the child must have a name.
"Name him for his father," said most of those who came.

I looked up at my dear Mary, who would not leave my side,
We both knew the proper name, and I spoke it out with pride.

"We'll call him John," I told them, and I kissed his little hand
"That's foolishness," my cousin said. "I fail to understand."

"You should not name him by yourself. I am glad I came!
The father of this baby boy must let us know his name!"

He said, "no person has that name, in your family line.
You should call him Zechariah. Let's ask him for a sign!"

They brought to Zechariah the tools to write his choice.
He smiled and started writing, though he had no voice.

He looked at me and smiled again, then handed them the note,
"We will call this boy child, John," was what he proudly wrote.

In that moment Zechariah found his voice restored,
A little scratchy in his throat, he began to praise the Lord!

"Out of the house of David, a savior will be raised,
Bringing rescue and salvation, for which He shall be praised!"

"John will be a prophet and he'll have great things to say.
He'll go out before the Holy One, and prepare the way."

All our friends and family, stared as he spoke on,
Foretelling all the future life, of his newborn son.

I looked into Mary's eyes, and Mary smiled at me,
For he had told the secret that was known by only three.

And yet these people didn't see, her secret was still safe,
Going back to Nazareth, there were things that she must face.

She would have to trust, and know her safety was the Lord,
That God would arrange her future, according to His word.

The two of us were blessed by God, to now raise up our son,
For Mary's Child must surely walk, in the way prepared by John.

The angel stood in front of us; saying, "Do not be afraid,
I bring you tidings of great joy about a newborn Babe."

*10 And the angel said unto them, Fear not: for, behold, I bring you
good tidings of great joy, which shall be to all people.
11 For unto you is born this day in the city of David a Saviour, which
is Christ the Lord.*

Luke 2:10,11 KJV

THE LAMB

I am a tax collector; I live here in Jericho.
My father was a tax man too, many years ago.

Augustus Caesar ruled the world in my father's day.
Roman rule was everywhere, and taxes must be paid.

My father got his orders, to go to Bethlehem,
To collect a special tax, on all the Jewish men.

Each man had to register in his ancestral home,
And pay a tax they levied, for the benefit of Rome.

My father was of David's line; he was proud of this,
This trip to him was special, one he wouldn't miss.

Bethlehem was a little town, it would be overrun,
With visitors proclaiming that they were David's sons.

My father took me with him; I was ten years old,
He said that I could come along, if I did as I was told.

We arrived in Bethlehem and found a place to stay,
We were tired from walking on a busy road all day.

The inn was empty that first night, but next day filled by noon.
Tax men were always early, and could afford a better room.

Often people didn't like the way he made a living.
But my father said collecting, was better far than giving.

We decided where to put his booth, in the middle of the town,
Men could pay while passing by; we were easy to be found.

Walking back for supper, we passed by some grazing sheep.
A friendly lamb came up to me, that I wished were mine to keep.

They were ready at the inn, to serve our evening meal.
The food we had was very good; my thankfulness was real.

When we finished we were glad, that we had a place to stay.
Some people were still looking, as they had been all day.

Tired from walking, we both lay down and Father fell asleep,
While I lay thinking of the lamb I longed so much to keep.

I crept over to the window where I thought I heard a noise,
A man and wife stood by the door; he had a quiet voice.

I couldn't understand his words, but I knew why he was there,
The inns were overflowing now, and there was no room to spare.

I felt so sorry for this man, and his tired pretty wife,
I hoped someone could help them; someone who was nice.

Then they both began to smile, as though their need was met,
That's when I left the window, and I crawled back into bed.

I thought again about the lamb, and prayed it could be mine,
If I worked, and trusted God, this might come in time.

A lamb with gentle loving eyes, was waiting in my dream.
I played with it till I woke up; I was hearing someone sing.

I thought I was still dreaming, but my eyes were open wide!
The floor beneath my feet was cold, as I went to look outside.

Again, I pulled the shutters back, and gazed into the night,
Distant shepherds tended sheep, in an evening clear and bright.

Still the music filled my ears, like I had never heard before,
The music was calling out to me, I wanted to hear more.

I was a small boy for my age, I didn't look my years,
But I was good at climbing, and climbing brought no fears.

I scrambled out the window, and dropped down to the ground,
The music now was louder, and I hurried toward the sound.

I ran straight to where the shepherds watched their grazing sheep,
Perhaps they passed their time by singing, lest they fall asleep.

The shepherds were just watching sheep, beneath a starlit sky,
While I was hearing music, that spilled down from on high!

I was excited by the music, though the shepherds were at rest,
I understood enough to know, that I was very blessed!

I nearly ran when I saw a shining light appear,
I stared in wonder, while my heart almost stopped with fear.

I thought I would be blinded by the radiant light that poured,
Into our midst, where we could see an angel of the Lord.

The angel stood in front of us; saying, "Do not be afraid,
I bring you tidings of great joy about a newborn Babe."

"A Savior who is Christ the Lord, has been born tonight,
He is lying in a manger, and will bring the world great light."

Then the sky was full of angels, singing high above the ground,
Joyful music grew and swelled till the night was filled with sound.

When the angels left us, we could hear them singing still,
Then the group of shepherds, began to climb the hill.

I followed close behind them, to find this Savior of the earth.
I would see this Holy Child, who had just been given birth.

They walked quickly through the night, toward to the nearest stable,
I ran fast to stay with them, and somehow I was able.

Ahead of us I thought I saw, an opening to a cave,
It wasn't far from the inn, where we had come to stay.

A glowing star was lighting up Bethlehem that night,
Through the door into the cave, everything was bright.

The man I'd seen came out to us; his eyes were bright with tears,
He smiled, and talked about the babe, lying in the manger here.

The shepherds went into the cave, and knelt there in the hay,
I saw them fold their roughened hands and bow their heads to pray.

I pushed through till I was close; they hardly noticed me,
I gazed at Him and at His mother; His mother smiled at me.

The baby was so beautiful, tucked within His nest,
I couldn't look away from Him--just like all the rest.

When He opened up His eyes, it took my breath away,
He was looking straight at me, from His cradle in the hay.

I knelt there looking in His eyes, and all I saw was love,
All the love in Heaven, He had brought down from above.

And still I heard the angels singing, glorious songs of praise,
I knew that God was with us, there in that stable cave.

The shepherds went back to their flocks, praising God on high,
And I went too, looking back, wanting both to laugh and cry.

I walked slowly to the inn, the star shone very bright,
I climbed back into our room; and lay awake all night.

In the morning when my father rose from a restful sleep,
I know he thought that I would ask to have a baby sheep.

I still loved that snow white lamb, as I had when we first came,
But the Baby and the playful Lamb, now seemed to be the same.

I jumped up to help my father, and then we broke our fast,
I thought of all I'd seen and heard, first moment till the last.

My father hurried to his work, I ran along beside,
He liked to have me help him, I was his joy and pride.

I tried to do what father asked, and remember what to say!
Then I heard a quiet voice that asked how much to pay.

It was the man I'd seen last night, would he remember me?
I thought that it might happen, but it wasn't meant to be.

He smiled at us and paid his tax, and then he turned away,
I hoped the sum my father charged, was what he ought to pay.

It wasn't long till we returned to our home in Jericho,
There I learned my father's business, all there was to know.

I never owned a snow white lamb, but I somehow didn't mind,
I now possessed that wondrous night, that God led me to find.

I tried to tell my father, but he told me not to lie,
I tried to tell my mother, but she would look at me and sigh.

Now, I am a tax man, I've taken more than what is fair,
I tell myself I have to live, and that I shouldn't care.

But sometimes in the evening, I still think about that night,
And the music fills my senses, and the angels fill my sight.

Wherever did that Baby go? And is He now a man?
I would so love to find Him, and I think sometimes I can.

I've heard that there's a Prophet, a Man from Galilee,
I heard He's coming to our town. That's a Man I have to see!

He's known to be a man of God, so it may be He can say,
Where to find the grown up Child, where does He live today?

I knew the route that He would take, through our city streets,
I planned to wait along the way, to be sure that we would meet.

Soon I found my waiting place and took the greatest care,
But I was short and in a crowd, He couldn't see me there.

So I found a tree to climb, a spreading sycamore,
Now I'd have a look at Him, and catch His eye for sure.

Then as He passed beneath my perch, He looked straight up at me,
His eyes met mine and Heaven's love was there for me to see.

I looked long into His eyes, and all I saw was love,
Here stood the Savior of the world--the Messiah from above.

"Zacchaeus," He spoke softly, though His every word was clear,
"Zacchaeus, you come down. There are things you need to hear."

"Today, Zacchaeus, I'm coming, to your house to dine,
Invite your friends, prepare your house, put out food and wine."

He was smiling and I knew, my life could never be the same.
The Messiah had remembered me. He even knew my name!

Then I thought of all the men I had cheated in my life,
I must go NOW and pay them back, not just once--but twice!

All those years I longed to find the Child I'd seen that night,
And all those years He cherished me, and kept me in His sight.

I loved Him in His manger bed, and I knew He was the Lamb.
And now I know that precious Child is the Son of the great I AM.

Six large empty water jars were standing by the wall,
"Fill these jars with water now. Go and fill them all."

*6 And there were set there six waterpots of stone, after the manner of
the purifying of the Jews, containing two or three firkins apiece.
7 Jesus saith unto them, Fill the waterpots with water. And they filled
them up to the brim.*

John 2:6,7 KJV

THE WEDDING AT CANA

My sister, Hannah, was betrothed about a year ago,
Caleb fell in love with her, and told our father so.

Caleb said that Hannah was the prettiest girl he'd seen,
He said that he would serve her, as though she were his queen.

He asked to marry Hannah, and take her as his wife,
We all thought the two of them would have a happy life.

The betrothal was completed; they shared the cup of wine,
The couple would be joined for life, at the proper time.

She asked me to be a bridesmaid; in all she had chosen ten,
We looked forward to her wedding day, with family and friends!

The months passed by quickly, as wedding plans were made,
The families got acquainted; the bridal price was paid.

Caleb's family lived in Cana, and we dwelt in Nazareth,
All of Hannah's family, would be the bridegroom's guests.

Both families were excited, as the wedding day drew near,
I asked for Cousin Mary's help; she said I need not fear.

Mother was at Hannah side, so Mary helped me dress,
Soon all the bridesmaids gathered, and I waited with the rest.

When darkness fell, I lit my lamp. I had extra oil with me.
It would be a night procession, and we we'd need the light to see!

We talked awhile and then we drowsed, and finally fell asleep,
We woke to see our lamps gone out; the night was black and deep.

With added fuel, our lamps grew bright, all of them but five,
Those girls began to beg for oil, to keep their flames alive.

"No," I told them sadly, "I cannot give you mine,"
"Go and purchase what you need, if you still have time."

They ran off to buy more oil, to find merchants who would sell,
Then we heard the bridegroom coming, and an eager silence fell.

The groom had arrived from Cana, six long miles away,
He was eager to fetch his Hannah, and take her home to stay.

Caleb's face shone with joy! And he nearly burst with pride!
He had a mount which his beloved, Hannah, was to ride.

We went inside the bridegroom's house at the journey's end,
The wedding feast was waiting and they were ready to begin.

While the family greeted Caleb and the lovely bride he won,
I was glad to see our Mary smile as she embraced her Son.

Jesus was there, and with Him came, some of His best friends,
I hoped He'd stay in Nazareth and live at home again.

Jesus is a carpenter, His father taught Him as a boy,
And now it seems He's come back home, to His mother's joy.

The wedding meal was wonderful, the wine was of the best,
I heard Jesus thanking Caleb, along with all the rest.

The party went on for hours; we had waited for this date,
Caleb's love for Hannah, was a cause to celebrate.

Then we noticed something wrong, a problem that was new,
We heard a servant ask the steward to tell him what to do.

I looked at Cousin Mary, then at the steward's face,
This Master of the party seemed to be amazed.

"The skins have burst," the servant said. "All the wine is lost!
There is no wine to be had tonight--not at any cost!"

There was panic in the servant's voice, that both of us could hear,
"Of course there's wine. Go look again." The steward voiced no fear.

Mary's face was thoughtful, as she glanced across the room,
Those drinking cups must be filled, and it needed to be soon.

Mary left our table; I saw her looking for her Son,
I followed close behind her, to see what could be done.

Jesus joined His mother, taking both her hands in His,
He smiled at her in greeting, and gave her cheek a kiss.

"My dear Son," she said to Him. There was firmness in her tone.
"We have a situation here, that they cannot fix alone."

"The skins have burst; there is no wine, and dinner must go on.
There will be festivities, until the coming dawn."

"This is our Hannah's wedding! The start of her new life!
Caleb must serve the finest wine, to honor his new wife."

Mary looked up at her Son; she was pleading with her eyes.
He seemed to be deciding, and she awaited His reply.

"My hour, Mother, has not yet come, why are you asking me?
The master servant is in charge here. Do you not agree?"

He was looking kindly, into His mother's eyes,
Then He gently smiled at her, and she gave a little sigh.

She slowly turned and softly called, to the servants standing near,
They came close to understand, what she wanted them to hear.

She gestured toward her tall young Son, standing by her side,
"Just do exactly as He says, and the wine will be made right."

Six large empty water jars were standing by the wall,
"Fill these jars with water now! Go and fill them all."

They filled up the water vessels, just as Jesus said to do.
I didn't see how this could help, but I thought that Mary knew.

"Draw some out now," Jesus said. "for the master of this feast."
A servant did as he was bid, though his worry seemed increased.

We watched the steward as he slowly sipped a little wine.
"The is the best!" he said, surprised. "This is very fine!"

Next, he spoke to Caleb, amazement in his voice.
"Most people serve out early, the finest and the choice."

"Even though the first you served, was good I will allow,
You held back your very best, and waited until now!"

"This wine that you saved back for us, is wonderful to taste,
Now that our meal is finished, let us savor without haste."

Caleb smiled in quiet pride, his joy was now complete,
He could take his lovely bride, and make a quick retreat.

The loving couple left us then, to spend a private night,
The party just continued on, and would till morning's light.

I looked at Mary and her Son, as they shared a secret smile,
She knows He's very close to God, she's known for quite a while.

I've heard many things from Mary, and truth shone in her eyes,
Turning jars of water into wine, brought her no surprise!

For years our people waited, for the Christ who was to come,
I hear a whisper in my soul, that our Jesus is The One.

Jesus' friends and followers, realizing what they saw,
Are looking at their Master, and their faces show their awe.

I don't think that He'll go home again, to Nazareth to live.
I think the world is waiting for all He has to give!

Here at my sister's wedding, a miracle has been done!
I wonder what will happen! I want to watch what's just begun!

"Put out again onto the lake, go where the water's deep.
Let down your nets, and there will be, a harvest there to reap."

*Now when he had left speaking, he said unto Simon, Launch out into
the deep, and let down your nets for a draught.*

Luke 5:4   KJV

COME AND FOLLOW

I fell deep in love with Simon when I was just thirteen,
I thought he was the kindest man I had ever seen.

He let me come aboard his boat, I helped him with the net.
He hardly even noticed me, much to my regret.

He was tall and very strong, with laughter in his eyes,
The kind of smile that left this girl with many dreaming sighs.

He asked my father for my hand, when I was seventeen,
I thought I'd die of happiness! I was in a dream.

And so my Simon married me, and we started our new life.
I knew I never would regret becoming Simon's wife.

Simon and his brother loved going out to fish,
Sunlight on an open sea, was all that they could wish.

Our marriage brought no babes to us, but we kept on in prayer,
That the Lord would someday favor us, and give a child into our care.

Mother was left to live alone when my father passed away,
First she came visit us, and then she came to stay.

Our lives went on quite smoothly when the nets were full of fish,
We prepared for empty nets, so we'd have no empty dish.

I walked one day to the shore, with a basket lunch in hand,
Simon would be starving, when his feet once hit the sand.

Simon, with his brother's help, brought in their empty craft.
They looked disheartened and so tired, that I didn't even ask!

They took the nets and began to wash and make repairs,
Weary now, and blurry eyed, they worked away their cares.

I watched a crowd approaching, and they gathered on the shore,
Listening as a Rabbi taught! They seemed eager to hear more.

The people crowded close to Him, till He had no place to stand,
So He climbed in Simon's boat, and was pushed away from land.

He paused to thank my Simon, then kept speaking loud and clear.
Everyone seemed mesmerized, and His voice reached every ear.

When the Rabbi finished talking, the crowd began to walk away,
He looked around for Simon, and He had some words to say.

"Put out again onto the lake where the water's deep.
Let down your nets, and there will be, a harvest there to reap."

Simon's smile was tired, when he heard and understood,
Even though he'd worked all night, he nodded that he would.

"We fished the lake all night long, and we've caught nothing yet.
Still you say to do this, Lord, so we'll go let down our net."

I wondered why they had agreed, as they pushed out on the lake,
Very soon the nets were dropped, for the Rabbi's sake.

It seemed I had watched them there, hardly any time at all,
When Andrew and my Simon, began to wave and call.

They were trying in the distance, to pull in their heavy net.
They were doing what they could, but they needed more help yet.

I watched in great excitement, as James and John put out,
They loved to share a heavy catch; no longer did they doubt.

I could see that Simon's boat sailed low and near to sinking,
They had better get help soon! The others shared my thinking.

James and John, the Zebedee's, were helping out their friends,
Both boats were full of wriggling fish and there seemed to be no end.

When those heavy loaded boats had finally reached the shore,
Simon fell at the Rabbi's feet, saying "Go away, my Lord."

"Please go!" he said, "and leave me here. For I am a sinful man.
I don't deserve these blessings, that are falling from your hand."

"Simon, do not be afraid. Just watch and wait and see,
From now on you'll fish for people. Come and follow me."

Simon and Andrew beached their boat, and so did James and John,
Before I knew what had happened, they had followed and were gone.

Simon kissed me quickly, before he walked away,
Hanging onto every word the Rabbi had to say.

I stood there wondering what to do; how long would he be gone?
Zebedee handed me a fish, and said we must carry on.

"Simon and the other men must do what they must do,
He'll be back and while he's gone, I'll sell those fish for you."

I thought that he'd be home to eat, I prepared that lovely fish,
Then I made some barley cakes, and arranged them on a dish.

I waited dinner for a while, then sat down and ate with mother,
We hadn't lost our appetite, without Simon and his brother.

When two weeks had come and gone, and he had not returned,
I wondered what the Rabbi taught; what lessons Simon learned?

Simon was not a scholar; his whole life was catching fish.
How could the Rabbi use him, was this really Simon's wish?

I tried not to be alarmed, and keep my soul in peace,
But I grew angry and uncertain, and felt my fear increase.

Mother tried to calm me, with soothing words and kind,
That Simon didn't love me, seemed to echo in my mind!

Then I didn't think of Simon, for my mother had grown ill,
She was burning with a fever, and was lying deathly still.

I prayed she would get better, that her fevered brow would cool,
She lay quiet and unmoving, beneath her cloak of woven wool.

I sat beside her all day long, and then all through the night,
She lay fevered and unconscious at the morning's light.

As dawn broke on the Sabbath day, I could not leave her side,
And since Simon was still absent, I just broke down and cried.

I watched her for some sign of change, and in my heart I prayed,
Then I started blaming Simon, and I wished so much he'd stayed!

Outside the house there were sounds, and soon I heard his voice,
Simon had come back to me, he must have made a choice!

I hurried to the door, both angry and relieved,
I had a lot to tell him, and I must be believed!

But when he caught me in his arms, I melted into tears,
I told him of my mother's state, and I told him of my fears.

Through sobs I talked to Simon, I made him realize,
If Mother's fever didn't break, surely she would die.

A little noise and I looked up, and saw Rabbi Jesus there,
His eyes were gentle and concerned, as though He really cared.

Andrew, James and John came walking through our door.
They were looking hard at Simon. They wanted to know more.

"My mother has a fever," I knew my voice was shaking.
"I've prayed to God all night long, but she simply isn't waking."

Rabbi Jesus came to me, and took my hand in His,
"Do not fear," He gently said. "Your mother will yet live."

Tears were streaming down my face, and hurt was in my soul,
He was good at finding fish. Could He make my mother whole?

I took Him in to see my mother, where she lay white as death,
Her only movement coming when she tried to catch her breath.

Jesus gently took her hand, and she opened up her eyes,
She raised her head and looked around, as though taken by surprise.

Color came into her face and she began to speak out loud,
"Why am I sleeping in my bed, when our house has such a crowd?"

"Please, all you hungry men--! Please leave my sleeping room!
I am coming to serve the food! I'll be with you very soon!"

She took Jesus' offered hand and soon was on her feet.
"All those men are famished. Let's put out food to eat!"

She followed the men out of the room. I was there with Him alone.
I understood now Who He was, and I needed to atone.

I thanked Him for my mother's health, kneeling at His feet.
He had given her new life, and He had forgiven me.

I told Him how I missed my Simon, and wanted him at home.
But I could stay here with my mother, I would not be alone.

"There's much that Simon has to learn. I need him for a while.
He will become a mighty rock," Jesus told me with a smile.

"Have you suffered any lack, while Simon was with me?"
"Our needs were always met," I said, "by our neighbor, Zebedee."

"I have called Simon Peter to come and follow Me.
He will come back to you again. Be patient and you'll see."

I knew that Jesus had a plan that must be carried out.
Now my Simon had to help him; this I did not doubt.

So when Simon went away again, to follow his dear Lord,
I found that I could smile and wait. He had given me His word.

I let him go and every day their safety was my prayer,
Whenever they came home to rest, I loved to have them there.

I didn't know He'd be arrested and then be crucified,
Or that my Simon would be untrue! He gave into fear and lied.

Three times he denied the Master, as a Man he didn't know,
But looking into Jesus' eyes, he heard the cock begin to crow.

Simon said he nearly drowned, in tormented fear and shame,
He hadn't been a rock for Jesus, so he couldn't keep this name.

The joy of Resurrection brought his sorrow to an end,
Simon was forgiven, and Jesus welcomed back His friend.

He ascended to His father, and we wept that He was gone.
The Holy Spirit brought us joy, and gave us strength to carry on.

My Simon now came home to me, and claimed me as his wife,
We vowed that we'd stay together till the ending of our life.

I cared faithfully for Mother, through her waning years,
We lifted one another up, and dried each other's tears.

Simon Peter did become, a rock on which to build,
I grew strong like Simon, we both were Spirit-filled.

That was many years ago, Jesus meant the things He said.
We both have followed, through the years, wherever He has led.

Now, we are here together, we have made our way to Rome.
I do not think we'll stay here long, for God will call us home.

The litter, now with ropes attached lowered Aaron down,
Those below were watching now, and hardly made a sound.

And when they could not come nigh unto him for the press, they un-
covered the roof where he was: and when they had broken it up, they
let down the bed wherein the sick of the palsy lay.

Mark 2:4 KJV

THE ROOF

Aaron is afraid of heights, and has been since a child.
To have to climb a ladder, will take away his smile.

I love the way that Aaron smiles, I love his curly hair.
I fell in love with Aaron, but I thought he didn't care.

Aaron liked another girl, before he asked for me,
That was ended long ago, as far as I could see.

Last year he spoke with father, and asked him for my hand.
We could share his parents' home and work their plot of land.

We would share his father's house. They would add a room.
He said that this would happen, someday very soon.

Father asked me how I felt, and said I could make the choice.
Would I marry Aaron, or prefer some other boy?

Of course, to marry Aaron and then be Aaron's wife,
Was what I wanted more than anything in life!

And so my father smiled at me, giving his consent.
Our families would be joined! I was sure that this was meant!

Preparations were begun; the bridal price was paid.
Aaron's father was ready and building plans were made.

It wasn't long till I could see, our room was taking shape.
Each morning I would think of Aaron when I came awake.

Sometimes, when I talked to Aaron, I'd look up and see,
Aaron was looking far away and not even hearing me.

But then he'd turn to me and smile, and I would melt inside,
Still I sometimes wondered, what it was he tried to hide.

The walls went up quickly, and then the floor went down,
It only lacked a roof now, and windows all around.

The evening came when they began to construct the roof,
I saw my Aaron's face go pale. He couldn't hide the truth.

I stood and watched while Aaron, began this fearsome task.
He wanted someone there to help, but I knew he wouldn't ask.

The beams were laid across the room, and reached from wall to wall,
And then a frame to hold the weight so the roof tiles would not fall.

Aaron worked and then relaxed. It seemed he'd faced his fear.
The evening's work was finished and quitting time was near.

I stood and watched the progress; soon he would descend.
We could rejoice together, as the project neared its end.

He approached the ladder. The roof was nearly done.
He would be coming down now. His battle had been won!

And then his younger brother tripped and took a fall,
He bumped against the ladder and knocked it from the wall.

I tried to shout a warning, but Aaron didn't look around,
He stepped back onto nothing, and fell down to the ground.

Aaron didn't strike the ground, he fell across a rock,
A stony shelf that held their tools, so they didn't have to walk.

I stood there, frozen, for a time, he was lying in a heap!
Then, I quickly ran to give him aid; he lay still as if asleep.

His body was twisted strangely, on his head I saw a bruise,
His eyes were closed and I was afraid we had no time to lose.

I cried out in fear as we all looked closely at his head.
His father carried him inside, and placed him on a bed.

Aaron didn't seem awake; he murmured senseless words.
He spoke the name of another girl, or that was what I heard.

His father quickly glanced at me, for he had heard this too.
Then he turned back to his son to see what he could do.

When Aaron was at last awake and clear in his own head,
He found he could not move his legs, nor could he leave his bed!

Next day I sat by Aaron, praying God would make him well,
Wanting back the Aaron he'd been before he fell.

In a while, our Aaron was sound and clear in mind,
But the Aaron who could work, was in another time.

At first he seemed quite happy when I was by his side,
Later, nothing pleased him, no matter how we tried.

"Go away," he said one day. "I am no good for you.
We cannot ever marry now, you know that this is true."

"I cannot help my father. I can't support a wife.
I cannot ever marry you. I no longer have a life."

I looked at him in sadness, tears ran down my face,
I told him that to be his wife, was my rightful place.

I said that I would stay, my future was with him,
I said that to leave him now would surely be a sin.

He turned away in anger, and would not look at me,
Still, I came there every day to help his family.

All the days moved slowly, and I prayed that he'd get well,
Aaron seemed so hopeless. He had been since he fell.

And then one day a Prophet came, a man we'd heard about.
He was staying in the village, at a neighbor's house.

Many people here in town, and some from far away,
Had come to find a healing, and to hear what He would say.

So I went to listen, when I'd done my morning chores,
Aaron's mother came along; we were eager to learn more!

As we watched and listened; an idea came and grew,
Aaron must see Jesus! This was something we could do!

She ran to find his father, and I went home to mine!
Jesus must heal Aaron while there still was time!

"Aaron!" I cried out to him, as we came into his house,
"We have found a Healer! We will take you to Him now!"

29

The put him on a pallet, our fathers and their friends,
I was so excited, for I was sure how this would end.

They carried him to the house where Jesus was inside,
I knew Aaron would be well again, and I would be his bride!

The house was full of people, crowded out into the street,
But Aaron must be brought inside, and placed at Jesus' feet.

The men were looking all around. There had to be a way!
If they continued waiting there, they could wait all day!

Aaron's father pleaded, with the people gathered round,
"Please, let me bring my son inside! He can be made sound."

Some people smiled and let them through, most of them did not.
How could they ever get inside, bearing Aaron on the cot?

Then someone pointed to the roof and Aaron's father grinned,
"We'll take him up and let him down! We will get him in!

I looked into Aaron's face and saw terror in his eyes,
His skin was white and I could feel his awful fear of heights.

Still, he didn't protest, as his father and his friends,
Led the way up the steps, toward his journeys end.

Aaron gripped the litter as they bore him up the stairs,
Though he slid around a bit, his friends had taken care.

They settled him there on the roof, above where Jesus taught,
An opening must now be made; a lowering point was sought.

Aaron's father gave the orders to carry out his plan,
Roof tiles soon gave way to their tools and clawing hands.

And now poor Aaron must be lowered to the floor below,
Some folks were staring up at them, while others didn't know.

The litter, now with ropes attached, lowered Aaron down,
Those below were watching now, and hardly made a sound.

I hurried down the outside steps and pushed my way inside,
I wanted to be close to him. "Let me through!" I cried.

Some of them moved a bit, and I pushed my way right through,
Till I was next to Jesus' men, and I could see what He would do.

Some people seemed to be amazed, others laughed out loud,
Jesus saw the gaping hole, and started laughing with the crowd.

Then He looked down at Aaron, and saw his hopeful eyes.
I prayed in desperation that He'd give Aaron back his life.

Then Jesus once again looked up, where our fathers now gazed down,
They looked so happy and so pleased, with the method they had found.

Jesus smiled at Aaron as he lay there on his bed,
He glanced up at our fathers, and then he clearly said,

"Your sins, my friend, are forgiven. You may start anew."
Relief was plain in Aaron's face. His father saw it too.

I saw some teachers standing by, along with some Pharisees,
"Did you hear that?" they were murmuring. "That is blasphemy!"

"You say I can't forgive his sins. You murmur and you talk.
Would it be easier if I said, "Take up your bed and walk?"

"So that you know I have the right, to forgive his sins,
I tell you now, Young Man, arise; be wholly well again."

"Go on home, my friend," He said, "and take your bed with you."
Aaron shouted when he heard this, but he was crying too!"

Laughing and crying together, Aaron scrambled to his knees,
And then a moment later, he was leaping to his feet!

Praising God, and singing, he took his bed up off the floor,
He put one arm around me, as he walked me to the door.

"My sins have been forgiven! I am a newborn man!
Look at me--I'm walking!" And then he kissed my hand.

"Now our room is finished and I want you for my wife,
I want you to be there with me, each day of my life."

Then he stopped and turned to me and took my hand in his,
"I need to tell you how I sinned. I have to tell you this."

"The girl I knew before you--I asked her to marry me.
Her father refused my offer, why I could not see!

I was hurt and angry when I asked to marry you,
I thought they would be sorry, if I found someone new.

I really didn't love you; I thought I never could,
I only asked to marry you, because Father said I should.

But you came and stayed by me, when there was nothing left,
You never turned away from me, no matter what I said.

Now I know I love you, I want you to marry me.
But knowing what I've told you, are you wanting to be free?

Jesus forgave me all my sins. I was haunted by my lie.
Can you forgive me also, and let the past go by?

I thought about that other girl and how he'd wanted her,
That he might still love her, caused my heart to stir!

Then I remembered Jesus; that he knew my Aaron's heart,
If Jesus gave forgiveness, then I could do my part.

"Yes," I whispered to him. "Aaron, yes I can.
I truly love you Aaron. You've grown into a man."

I knew we'd follow Jesus, all He said, we'd do,
He'd given Aaron back to me. He made us both brand new.

And so our marriage date was set, our future was in sight,
Aaron has finished with the roof. He's not afraid of heights.

Peter sank into the waves where he floundered and went down,
"Lord, save me now!" Peter cried. "Please save me or I'll drown."

*30 But seeing the wind, he became frightened, and beginning to sink,
he cried out, "Lord, save me!"
31 Immediately Jesus stretched out His hand and took hold of him,
and *said to him, "You of little faith, why did you doubt?"*

Matthew 14:30,31 KJV

COURAGE TO WALK

They used to call me Levi; now Matthew is my name.
I have a younger brother, and he is known as James.

Our Lord and Savior, Jesus, called my brother first.
He was the younger and the better. I know I was the worst.

I've been a tax collector since I became a man.
I was hired and trained by Rome to do the best I can.

My pay was good and I lived well, though I wasn't much admired,
But my easy life was not enough, and my soul grew very tired.

As middle age came onto me, I grew depressed and bored.
Did I have the courage to walk with my brother's Lord?

James so loved to speak of Jesus, that in Him I'd find rest.
For my soul there would be peace, and through Him I'd be blessed.

In time, I began to listen, to my little brother, James,
When he spoke about his precious Lord, and how his life had changed.

One day while working at my booth, close to the city gate,
I cursed the wine I drank last night, that caused my head to ache.

I looked up from my pens and scrolls, and saw a group of men,
Approaching my collection booth; they paused, and I saw Him.

Jesus was looking straight at me, and I saw He understood,
The pain that I was suffering, and my tired and bitter mood.

Brother James caught my eye, and gave me a little smile,
As though he knew my mood would change, in just a little while.

I felt the Master watching me! Did He know my sins and lies?
"Come, follow Me," was all He said, as He looked into my eyes.

I found the courage to walk away, leaving everything behind.
I'm sure the people paying taxes, were glad I lost my mind!

As I approached the Master, tears were rolling down my face,
He put His arms around me, in His welcoming embrace.

"Matthew, I am glad you've come. I need your helping hand.
I have a job for you to do, that you will come to understand."

My head no longer gave me pain; my heart felt young and light.
I said aloud that I had never seen, a day so clear and bright!

I led them all back to my home! I had so much to share!
I sent out word to all my friends to come to dinner there.

Never before in all my life, had I given such a feast!
I gladly welcomed everyone--the greatest to the least!

A crowd of tax collectors came, and people mired in sin,
All the doors were open! All who wanted could come in.

I ordered mounds of food prepared, set out to feed our guests.
Some found life as well as food; through Jesus they were blessed.

I urged Jesus and his friends, to stay and rest a while.
I gave away my household goods, and that made Jesus smile.

Jesus taught truth in parables, unlike the Pharisees,
Then, He explained the stories, and His words were clear to me.

I am an educated man, and I understand the law,
Years ago I turned my back on the hypocrites I saw.

Pharisees came quickly forth, with angry criticism,
When He sat down at table, and ate with those in sin.

Finally, I heard them speak, as they looked Him in the eye,
Saying, 'this is strange behavior, and we demand you tell us why'.

"Physicians," He replied, "are not sent to healthy men.
It's the sick who need a doctor, and to them I must attend."

"I have not come to call the righteous, but those who are in sin,
Those who are most burdened down, are those who will come in."

I heard His words with thankfulness; he was positive and sure,
My sinful past was something, I no longer need endure!

The Master and His followers, left my house one day,
I found the courage to leave my home, and join Him on His way.

The Master had included me, in His group of closest friends,
My dream was to walk with Him, until my life would end.

We walked through wind and weather, many miles across our land,
Through villages and valleys, through the dust or sand.

I wasn't used to walking, so many miles each day,
My feet were sore and blistered, but I would not cause delay.

I saw so many wondrous things, I began to write them down!
Jesus saw my written notes, and was pleased with what He found.

One disciple that I admired, more than all the rest,
That was Simon Peter! He could pass the toughest test.

He was skilled with sailing boats, and water held no fears.
A troubled sea could make me ill, and bring me close to tears!

I loved to walk beside our Lord, wherever He might lead,
But I had a fear of water, and boats I did not need.

So when He fed five thousand men, on the hills beside the sea,
Where we were going after that, had just occurred to me.

The Master called us all together, and told us what to do,
We must cross the sea without him, with Peter and his crew.

Evening now was drawing on, the light had begun to fade.
Jesus turned and walked away; He would not be delayed.

I followed Peter to the boat, and they helped me climb aboard,
Simon Peter was in charge, in the absence of our Lord.

I had sailed on Peter's craft, through rough and stormy seas,
But Jesus had been there with us, and my fearful heart was eased.

The sea at first was smooth as glass, and I drew an easy breath,
Within an hour the sky was dark, and I saw we'd have no rest.

Soon the breeze had freshened, till a mighty wind was blowing,
Billowing sails were snapping, and I saw the waves were growing.

Somehow we would make it, though I shook with fear and cold,
I'd likely face much worse than this, before I had grown old.

The next wave lifted up the bow, and I rolled to the stern!
If Peter had no fear of storms, how did he ever learn?

Now I saw that all the crew, had terror in their eyes,
Even Peter seemed afraid, and I clung harder in surprise!

We held fast to what we could, while the small craft tossed about,
The wind was howling in our ears, and drowned out all my shouts.

I tried desperately to pray, but I was so filled with fear,
I tried to think of Jesus and I wished that He were here!

I kept my eyes on Peter. We had faced a storm before,
Mighty winds and heavy waves, far away from any shore!

Now Simon Peter was staring out, into the howling storm,
All our eyes followed his, where we could see a form.

"It's a spirit," someone cried, and so it did appear!
First a storm and now a ghost; was there yet more to fear?

Despite the wind that blocked my ears, I now made out His voice,
"It is I," I heard Him say, and I could feel my soul rejoice!

"Take courage," He was telling us, "Do not be afraid!"
I could see Him clearly now--answering the prayer I'd prayed.

With open mouth, Peter stared, as we barely stayed afloat,
Jesus was walking on the waves, coming to the boat.

"Lord, if it's truly you I see, and you are really there!
Bid me come onto the water. Just call me and I'll dare!"

"Come, Peter," was the answer, and Peter's faith seemed strong.
He climbed out on the water, as though nothing could go wrong!

The wind was hard against him and he was soaking wet,
He looked down into the water, and saw a deathly threat.

Peter sank into the waves where he floundered and went down,
"Lord, save me now!" Peter cried. "Please save me or I'll drown."

I saw Jesus was beside him; He answered Peter's shout,
"Oh, you of little faith," He said, as He lifted Peter out.

Jesus gripped Peter's hand, His arm round Peter's waist,
He led Peter to the boat, without any show of haste.

As they climbed into the craft, I saw the howling wind had died,
Now the sea was smooth like silk, with tiny waves like sighs.

Jesus came to save us when the storm was as it's worst.
"You truly are the Son of God!" Peter said it first.

Still shivering and shaking, we worshipped our dear Lord,
Thanking Him our lives were saved, and that He was on board!

It seemed to me that Peter, had come so very near,
He had walked on water, while love cast out his fear.

I thought somehow in Jesus' eyes, Peter passed a test,
He had done what I would not, nor would all the rest.

When I left to follow Jesus, I thought I gave my all,
I didn't know I'd kept my fears, and fear could make me fall.

Jesus came to save us, He was sent down from above,
On that stormy night at sea, I was baptized in His love.

Jesus' hand touched Jairus' arm, and He smiled at Jairus' wife,
"Come with Me now and you will see she has not departed life."

And all wept, and bewailed her: but he said, Weep not; she is not dead,
but sleepeth.

Luke 8:52 KJV

JAIRUS' DAUGHTER

Leah is my closest friend; she's gentle and she's kind.
Leah is a quiet girl, while I'm quick to speak my mind.

We spend our time together, when all our work is done,
Our mothers' smile and tell us to go and have some fun.

We know we have to work at home, when the afternoon is bright,
To help prepare the food to serve, at the fading of the light.

Three days ago the sun was hot, so we walked along the shore,
Leah took her sandals off; her blistered heel was sore.

We walked into the cool blue lake, holding up our skirts,
I told Leah this might help her blistered foot that hurt.

We waded for a long time, much longer than we should.
The cooling water of the lake made us both feel good.

With surprise we saw before us the setting of the sun,
It was dinner time at home, the day was nearly done.

We knew we had to hurry back, for we were very late,
Our sandals had gone missing; we were in a frantic state.

Scrambling, with wet bare feet, we searched the rocky shore,
Till I turned to look for Leah, but she wasn't by me any more.

I called to her and hurried back, to where my friend was lying,
Her ankle turned, her foot was cut, and I saw that she was crying.

I helped her up to lean on me, then slowly we walked on,
We met our fathers coming out, to discover where we'd gone.

Leah's face was wet with tears, and she bit her lip in pain,
I knew that I had caused it all, I wished I could explain.

Jairus lifted up his daughter, concern was on his face.
My father was more stern with me, and I was in disgrace.

I ate my waiting dinner, and helped put away the dishes,
Tomorrow I must work all day, no matter what my wishes.

I kissed my mother and my father, and went quickly to my bed,
I knew I should have paid more heed, to all the things they said.

Now my friend had injuries, and healing would take time,
We would not be together much, and deep regret was mine!

When I arose next morning, I went quickly to my chores,
First, I prayed for Leah, hoping Mother now knew more.

"Mother, how is Leah?" I queried, as we sat to rest,
"This is mostly all my fault. I'm so sorry," I confessed.

"My child, you knew that it was wrong to make your family wait,
Then you ran barefoot in the dark, when you found that you were late!"

"We'll go later to see Leah, when all our work is done,
No one blames you for her hurt, but in future watch the sun."

When we entered Leah's house, we didn't see her there,
Her mother said she was asleep; she needed rest and care.

For Leah's foot was swollen, and the skin was hot and pink,
Her mother seemed distracted as she mixed a healing drink.

I told her I was sorry, but she didn't seem to understand,
She looked at me and smiled, and quickly squeezed my hand.

My mother told her softly, that we all would trust and pray,
That Leah would be better soon, and soon might be today.

But Leah wasn't better; she was much worse by night,
When I stood there by her bed, I swallowed down my fright,

Leah burned with fever, while her mother bathed her skin,
I whispered that I loved her; I was weighted down by sin.

Next day she was no better, she drifted and she dreamed,
I only saw her from the door, but that was how it seemed.

On the morning of the third day, I thought she must be well,
I went with Mother to her house, but even we could tell.

Leah didn't move or speak; her mother wept and prayed,
We sat down close beside her, and it was there that we both stayed.

Leah's father paced the room, and I could feel his fear,
Till mother said to Jairus, "I've heard that prophet's here."

"He arrived here yesterday; someone saw Him as He came.
If He could just touch Leah! He has healed the blind and lame!"

"Why don't you go and fetch him, and bring Him back with you,
He's healed so many others, perhaps He'll heal her too!"

Leah's mother also spoke, and her voice was choked with tears,
"Jairus, will you go and find Him? You must bring Him here."

Jairus stopped his pacing, and went to his daughter's room,
"Yes, " he said "I'll go right now, He can't get here too soon."

Jairus hugged his weeping wife; he spoke gently and with care.
"Stay beside her while I'm gone; make sure she knows you're there."

Their house began to fill, with neighbors and with friends,
Tears fell on my folded hands, as I prayed all this would end.

Leah's mother sat by Leah, in the nearby room,
The rest of us just waited, filled with growing gloom.

We thought that Jairus would perhaps, return within the hour,
As a leader in his synagogue, he could bring the Prophet's power.

We waited and we prayed, for an hour and then another,
Then the air was shattered, by the screams of Leah's mother.

Her closest friends gathered round, held her in their arms,
She was so consumed by grief, I thought she'd come to harm.

My father knelt by Leah's bed, his hand was on her wrist,
Next, he took a mirror, and put it gently to her lips.

Then he stood and turned away, sorrow in his face,
"The child is taken from us. There's no more need for haste."

I sat there in the corner, there was nothing I could do,
Someone was to blame for this, and only I knew who.

It wasn't long till we saw Jairus, as he entered in,
The Prophet walked beside him, followed by three men.

My father went to meet them, to tell them Leah died,
Jesus looked at our sad faces and He saw the tears we cried.

Jairus' grief showed in his eyes, as he held his weeping wife.
"My dear, my dear." he said to her, "We could not save her life."

The Prophet, Jesus, went to them. He said they must not weep.
"The girl's not dead at all, my friend. She simply lies asleep."

My father went and stood with them; he looked them in the eyes,
"I wish that what you say were true, but you don't realize,

Little Leah no longer lives, her heart no longer beats,
She does not breathe, and I tell you true! She is not asleep."

Jesus' hand touched Jairus' arm, and He smiled at Jairus' wife,
"Come with Me now, and you will see she has not departed life."

The three walked to Leah's room, followed by the Prophet's men.
We couldn't hear what they said, when the door had closed them in.

I looked sadly at my father; my father shook his head.
"I am so very sorry, child, but your little friend is dead."

We wondered what was happening, but expected nothing much,
No one believed that He could have such power in His touch.

It was just a little while till they opened up the door,
And Leah stood there smiling, as healthy as before.

"Give the girl some food," He said, "It's time to feed the child",
"I am hungry," Leah whispered, "I haven't eaten for a while!"

Leah's mother went for food, the rest seemed struck with awe,
I stood and stared at Jesus, so I'd remember what I saw.

Jairus gripped the Master's hand, his face glowed like the sun,
"When you touched her, life returned! You are the promised one!"

"Lord, how can we ever thank you! My words aren't good enough!"
"You're blessed by God," Jesus said. " Go now and share His love."

He walked slowly toward the door, and then He stopped by me,
He gently touched my cheek and said, "You're grieving, I can see."

"I am the one who sinned," I said. "I knew what we should do,"
"Be at peace," He said to me. "God has forgiven you."

He left the house and went away, taking his three men,
And with a light and joyous heart, I went to hug my friend.

Leah suffered awful things and all because of me,
But Jesus has forgiven, and healed my friend and me.

Then you would ask Me for a drink, and this is what I'd give--
Living water so you thirst no more, however long you live."

*Jesus answered and said to her, "If you knew the gift of God, and who
it is who says to you, 'Give Me a drink,' you would have asked Him,
and He would have given you living water."*

John 4:10 KJV

WOMAN AT THE WELL

I am a simple woman. I lead a simple life.
I do the things that must be done--and I am no man's wife.

I was married at sixteen to an older wealthy man,
He had no living children, but he did possess some land.

He passed away quite suddenly, after three long years,
They wed me to his brother, whose wife shed angry tears.

Our union brought no children, and he soon was tired of me,
His wife was glad to see me go, and I was happy to be free.

I went back to my parents house, and they took me in,
They blamed me that I'd been divorced, and spoke to me of sin.

Another marriage was arranged, though it was hard to do,
I was not so pretty now, though I worked hard it was true.

I was thirty years or more, when this husband passed away,
My parents were no longer living. I was on my own that day.

His property had come to me, as he had no other heir,
Very soon, I was wed again, to a man who seemed to care.

He squandered my inheritance, till all of it was gone,
When there was nothing left to spend, a light began to dawn.

I lost my temper and let him know, that I was through with giving.
He divorced me and I was left, with no way to earn a living.

Two years passed and I met a man, who was loving and most kind.
I married him though I really thought I must have lost my mind.

I worked hard and so did he, and it seemed this time I'd won.
Thieves killed him on a lonely road--as well as our young son.

I was through with marriage, but I wasn't through with men.
I needed help to live my life, so I began it all again.

Joab is an honest man, he works and earns good pay,
He comes home to me at night, and says he plans to stay.

He's asked me to marry him, though I am forty-four,
I don't want to marry him. I'll not marry any more.

We are respected in the village. We pay the debts we owe.
Some people say we live in sin, but I don't really know.

Village women walk to the well, when dawn has lit the sky,
I don't often go so early, and there are several reasons why.

I have had five unions, been divorced two times,
I refuse to marry Joab. My current life is fine.

Some of them have pity, and some of them have scorn,
I just feel I've seen it all, and now I'm tired and worn.

I don't want their pity, or their cold unfriendly stares,
So I go later to the well, when no one else is there.

So it was that fateful day, I walked to the well at noon,
To draw my jug of water. I'll dance to my own tune.

When I arrived at Jacob's well, a man was sitting there.
I saw He must be Jewish, by His prayer shawl and His hair.

"Will you draw Me a drink of water?" He asked me with a smile?
I stared at Him in wonderment, and was speechless for a while!

"Sir, I am Samaritan, as you can plainly see,
You want a drink of water, and you are asking me?"

I looked at Him and tried to guess if there was need for fear?
Jews don't speak to us at all, and they rarely pass by here.

He laughed out loud, and I thought He seemed so very kind,
"If you knew God's gift," He said, "and had this in your mind,

Then you would ask Me for a drink, and this is what I'd give--
Living water so you thirst no more, however long you live."

I was smiling as I answered, for He seemed the one in need,
"You have no means for drawing water, and this well is very deep!"

"Are you greater than the one who gave to us this well?
This came from our father, Jacob, and he drank from it himself!"

"Jacob's sons drank right here, as did his flocks and herds,
This well came down from Jacob, and it says so in the Word."

I got busy with my water jug, and filled it to the brim,
Then I took a serving cup, and gave a drink to Him.

"Drink this water," He softly said, "and soon you will need more,
Soon enough you'll thirst again, just as you did before.

Drink the water that I give, and you'll never thirst again.
Living water to satisfy, as no other water can."

He took the cup and drank from it and gave it back to me.
I thought that He was speaking truth; that it was plain to see.

"Give me this water, Sir," I said, "that I may thirst no more.
Coming to draw water here, is a tiring painful chore!"

"Go and get your husband, and bring him back with you",
He was asking me for something that I really could not do.

"I have no husband, Sir," I said. "I can't do what you ask!"
I did not explain to Him, why I could not complete this task.

"You say you have no husband, and this is surely true,
Yet you have had five husbands, and none are now with you ."

"You are living with a man to whom you are not wed,
He is not your husband, just as you have said."

I stared at Him and realized, He knew all the things I'd done!
He knew of all my marriages. He had not left out one.

"You are a prophet, Sir, I see! You know the details of my life."
You know I have no husband and I no longer am a wife."

"And since you are a prophet, I will ask you now,
Where we are to worship? Please tell me where and how!

We worship on Mt Gerazim; we've worshipped there for years,
Jews proclaim Jerusalem, and say we're wrong to worship here."

"The time will come," He said to me, "when you will not worship there,
Neither mountaintop nor Jerusalem, will be the place for prayer."

"A time is coming very soon; in fact, that time is here,
To worship in Spirit and in truth, and to let our God draw near."

God is spirit, and He loves those, who are Spirit filled,
The Spirit will lead you to the truth, as God, Himself, has willed.

I was excited by His words! He seemed to know so much!
"The Messiah will come," I told Him, "and explain this all to us!"

He smiled at that. His eyes were kind, and then He said to me,
"I--the One who speaks to you--I, Myself, am He."

To this I had no answer, so I stood and stared at Him.
I knew He was God's holy One, and I knew He saw my sin!

Like the Jews we've waited, for our Messiah to come,
And there He stood before my eyes, in the noonday sun.

Some friends of His came with food, and they joined Him there,
They seemed surprised He talked to me, but no one seemed to care.

I knew that what He said was true. I could feel it in my soul.
My friends and neighbors came to mind! They must all be told!

I left my jug of water there, and hurried back toward town,
I had to tell the people there, and spread the news around!

I told everyone I saw--met their disbelieving eyes.
I told them He knew everything, that had happened in my life.

Then I begged them just to come--to see and understand!
We had a prophet in our midst--the Messiah in our land!

"Come and meet this Prophet! You must come with me and see!
This is the One we've waited for--and He just talked with me!"

He knows our past and future, He can guide our feet,
He has this "living water" for which we all have need!

They followed me to find Him. He was still beside the well.
We listened to Him as He spoke, until the evening fell!

We urged Him to remain with us; He smiled and then agreed.
We offered food and lodging of which they were in need.

"God is our Father," He told us all. "And Holy is His Name.
We pray in spirit and in truth, then nothing is the same."

He told us how God cares for us, like the lilies in the field,
If we only will believe on Him, our eternal life is sealed.

He is our Messiah too! This we quickly understood.
Here was a Man who cared for us, as no other could.

Because of what I told my friends, some listened and believed,
But then they came to love Him, for the peace that they received.

Now I know that I have sinned, as I struggled on my way.
And now I know I can trust God, to lead me through each day.

Joab still says he loves and wants to marry me,
I'll live alone until I'm sure, that this is meant to be.

God will let me know if I'm meant to be his wife,
And I will follow Jesus till I depart this life.

I fell down at His sandaled feet, and shouted, "God, be praised!
Sir, I thank you for my very life! I am like a dead man raised!"

*15 Now one of them, when he saw that he had been healed, turned
back, glorifying God with a loud voice,
16 and he fell on his face at His feet, giving thanks to Him.*

Luke 17:15,16 KJV

THE THANKFUL ONE

I was born in Sychar, close to Jacob's well.
I loved the "Jacob stories" that my mother used to tell.

We worship on the mountain top. We're not like the Jews.
They try to stay away from us, but that is nothing new.

I joined my father's business, when I became full grown,
I knew that someday this would be, the business I would own.

My father and my mother, loved and cared for me,
They brought me up and trained me, very carefully.

At twenty-five, I wed the daughter of my father's friend,
We'd live our lives together and take what God might send.

I thought that we'd have children; sons to carry on the line,
Pretty little daughters, and I'd be proud that they were mine.

Then something happened to me, I didn't recognize at first,
But in a year I knew for sure, and I had to face the worst.

First it was a tingling, and my fingertips were numb,
I saw a patch on my arm, where pale light skin had come.

Sores appeared here and there, sores that would not heal,
I always had a running nose, that I couldn't even feel.

This all happened slowly; I thought that it would pass!
I thought it was a minor thing, and that it couldn't last.

All these little symptoms didn't pass and fade away,
Then I knew my disease, was real and here to stay.

First, I told my father all, and asked him what to do,
I knew that this would grieve him, but he must know the truth.

Father said he'd tell my mother, and I spoke to my wife,
The thing that had to happen would completely change my life.

They could no longer touch me, for the law was very clear,
I could not let myself bring harm, to the ones I held most dear.

Till my life was ended, I would suffer from this curse.
A leprous husband was a fate my wife did not deserve.

So I left the home I loved, my family and my friends,
And a writing of divorcement let my marriage end.

I knew that I must live alone, or in the company,
Of other people suffering from the curse of leprosy.

When I left my former life, I left the neighborhood,
I'd make myself dead to them, and manage as I could.

I took some coins along with me, to last me for a while.
I still had to feed myself, as I walked those lonely miles.

It wasn't long till I joined with a group of other men,
Living with their leprosy; together we were ten.

Some of them were far along, with hands becoming claws,
Some faces were disfigured, and some toes were nearly lost.

I still looked more normal, than these desperate hurting brothers.
I shared my coins and bought the food, for myself and for the others.

When I first joined these outcast men, I found myself repelled,
It wasn't long till I had changed all the views I held.

I did my best to care for them, what they would let me do,
My health was not so bad as theirs; my leprosy was new.

Some of them were Jews, and didn't like me much,
I always struggled to be kind, and keep a gentle touch.

I helped them wash their dirt away; we walked slowly lest they fall,
As long as I had coins to spend, I bought food to feed us all.

Serving these poor lepers brought me peace of mind,
I was now a leper too. How could I not be kind?

And so we went from day to day, and then from year to year.
Ringing the bell and walking, and knowing we brought fear.

My father helped us when he could, he'd come and seek me out,
He and my mother prayed to God, that my healing come about.

I knew there was no cure for me; I couldn't be made whole,
But helping fellow sufferers, gave me peace within my soul.

One day, my father came to find me, and told me something new,
There was a Healer near to us, whose name he even knew!

"This Teacher's name is Jesus! He came to our hometown!
Three days He stayed and taught us! He can still be found!"

"This Teacher heals the sick," he said. "I'm sure he can heal you!
You must go and seek Him! What I say to you is true!"

I thought Father was mistaken, and that he hoped too much,
He was listening to gossip; there was no such healing touch.

My companions listened eagerly to what my father had to say,
They cried out that we must seek Him--we must go without delay!

I looked at them, those wretched men; looked at them and wept,
I saw hope arise in desperate eyes; we would go when we had slept.

Morning came, we broke our fast, and I saw their eager faces!
We'd go now to seek Him out, to search the likely places!

We started walking toward the town where my father had directed,
I dreaded their hurt and broken hopes, if all went as I suspected.

We walked all day but saw no man, till late in the afternoon.
In the distance, we saw a group we would approach quite soon.

I was glad for these hurting men, who had trudged for weary miles,
They stumbled now on damaged feet, with faces wreathed in smiles.

When we were close, they called out loud, and I joined my voice with theirs,
"Jesus, Master, please have pity!" We were expecting cold hard stares!

I heard my father's words again, repeating in my mind,
Father said that He could heal us, if He chose to be so kind!

I shouted out my plea to Him, perhaps His power was real!
"Master, you can make me clean, if You only will!"

He raised His hand in greeting. He came up close and smiled.
"I will," He whispered softly. "Be clean. No longer be defiled."

"Go find a priest and show yourselves. You are healthy men.
Cleanse your bodies, go your way, you are well again."

I looked at all the others; they looked just the same,
So, we turned to go away, praying we were changed.

We walked along in silence to do as we were told,
When I noticed that my fingers were feeling warm, then cold.

I also noticed that my toes could feel the leather of my shoe,
I looked down at my hands, and saw the skin looked fresh and new.

I saw the lesions of my friends, fading fast before my eyes,
Strength and health were pouring in, was what I realized.

"He has healed us! We are whole!" I screamed my joy out loud.
"We are clean! Praise God above!" We all began to shout!

"He is a Prophet! I see it now! He is the Holy One!
This Man is our Messiah! The One who is to come!"

"I must go back and thank Him! I have to let Him know!"
These thoughts were tumbling in my mind as I turned to go!"

"We're going on," the others said. "Now that we are clean,
We will wash and find a priest! Our bodies must be seen!"

"You go back and thank Him. We must be traveling on.
We will seek and find a priest by tomorrow's dawn!"

I stared at them a little while, but I knew what I must do.
"I'm returning to the Master, so I take my leave of you.

I've grown so close to each of you; you'll always be my friends.
And now we're healed and well again, our closeness has to end."

I turned and walked away from them, tears ran from my eyes,
Such joy was welling up in me, it took me by surprise.

I must return to Jesus! I had to thank Him on my knees!
A healthy happy future life, spread out in front of me!

I ran all the way on healthy feet, back to Jesus and His men.
"My Lord," I cried as I came near. "Praise God! I'm clean again!"

I fell down in front of Him, and shouted, "God, be praised!
I thank you for my very life! I am like a dead man raised!"

He smiled at me, a happy smile, and His eyes began to shine.
"You are the leper that was here; where are the other nine?"

"All of you were lepers; nine I know were Jews.
I do not see the others, though they are clean as you."

"You are a Samaritan, and you're praising God above,
Your faith has made you whole again; go in peace and love."

I traveled back to Sychar and found my family waiting there,
I rejoiced to see my lovely wife! Now we have a life to share.

Leprosy had stolen years from the life I'd planned to live,
But I also learned the truest joy comes from what you give.

My life is good and I thank God, but I miss the other nine,
I wonder if they found our Lord, and I pray they will in time.

Jesus came to Sychar; He spoke and taught the Word,
As for me and my house, Jesus is our Lord.

He caught my eye and asked me then, "Do you want to get well?"
He must know I've wanted that, since that awful day I fell!

When Jesus saw him lying there, and knew that he had already been a
long time in that condition, He *said to him, "Do you wish to get well?"

John 5:6 KJV

THE HEALING POOL

I was born a favored child; my parents' only son.
My older sisters loved me, and every game I won.

My father was a wealthy man; he gained his wealth in trade.
He acquired flocks and herds, and a house that he displayed.

I traveled with my father, to many a distant shore,
I knew that in my future, great things were in store.

And so it was as I grew up, and so it still should be,
Until the day when my whole world, came to an end for me.

I was just eleven then; soon I would have twelve years,
Then I'd become a grown-up, with no more childish fears.

I threw caution to the winds, when I rode my father's horse,
A hissing snake, a sudden stop, and I was thrown, of course.

I pitched forward past his head, and lay helpless at his feet.
The life I knew was ended there, when I didn't keep my seat.

Father brought a doctor, for he could see I had great harm.
I couldn't move or feel my legs, and could hardly move my arms.

The doctor could do nothing. The damage had been done.
Mother tried to care for me--she would not give up her son!

And so my parents said, that there was one more thing to do.
We could go to the healing pool, like a man my father knew.

Bethesda, by the sheep gate, was where many had been cured,
If they were in the water first, when the angel came and stirred.

We journeyed to Jerusalem. This brought back my father's smile.
There he rented a house nearby, which we'd need for just a while.

They carried me to the water's edge, and there they laid me down.
They sat there with me all day long, lest I fall in and drown.

My eyes stayed on the healing pool, but it was still and clear,
I never saw a ripple, for no angel had come near.

I was tired and disappointed and my father was as well,
Still there would be tomorrow, and with angels, who can tell?

They brought me there every day, till several months had passed.
One day, I saw the water move, and knew the angel came at last!

The servants who were with me, were quick to put me in,
But I watched another leap in first, with no need for helping men.

He shouted praises as the water swirled around his painful limbs,
"Thank the Lord, I'm healed," he cried, and I thought I hated him!

I'll be next, I told myself. And my parents both agreed.
When the water stirred again, we'd be quicker with our need.

Watching that pool of water was all I did each day.
I wanted back the life I lost, and I hated this delay.

My father was beside himself; he had to have an heir;
A son to travel and to learn, the business he would share.

How long," he wondered, "must we wait, for God to intervene?
God would surely cure his son, when this desperate need was seen!

And so the days continued on, the months and then the years,
Every day was just the same, with the waiting, and the fears.

My father went back to his work, he traveled once again,
Instead of me he took with him, a helpful hired man.

My mother stayed close by my side, she prepared my favorite food,
She always prayed and trusted God, and kept a hopeful mood.

Each day, she thought, would be the day, that I would be made whole.
But after years beside the pool, her faith left me quite cold.

God seemed to have forgotten me, or perhaps He didn't care,
Others people got their healing, but for me He wasn't there.

Still, Father sent me every day, to lie waiting on my quilt,
I begged to go see something else, then I drowned in guilt.

As I grew older into manhood, I could not now believe,
That I'd be healed or have a life. I had surely been deceived.

Such bitterness had grown in me, since God took my life away,
I knew deep within my soul, that as I was, so I would stay.

My father died quite suddenly, when I was thirty years,
I was so angry deep inside, there was no room for tears.

And when my mother passed away, several years ago,
I stayed on my pallet by the pool. I had nowhere else to go.

My father's business now belonged to his hired man.
There was nothing there for me in his business plan.

My sister now took care of me, as my mother used to do,
I was just another child to her, and this I hated too.

My sister's sons now carried me, to the pool each day.
They would place me by the water, and that is where I'd stay.

If an angel stirred the water, I was always late,
Others got their healing, all I had was hate.

Almost forty years I lay, beside the healing pool.
I looked back and knew I'd been, nothing but a fool.

I often wished I'd died that day, I fell off my father's horse,
Like any other wish I had, I couldn't die, of course.

One day a Man came to the pool, and stopped to look at me.
He was a total stranger. I wondered what He came to see.

"This man here," someone said, "has been waiting many years,
To be first into the water, when the angel comes and stirs."

He met my eyes and I could feel Him looking in my mind.
I turned away because I knew, all the anger He would find.

He caught my eye and asked me then, "Do you want to get well?"
He must know I've wanted that, since that awful day I fell!

I've come here nearly every day, for almost forty years,
Does He think that I enjoy, lying bored and helpless here?

"No one will help me to the pool, when the water's stirred,
While I'm still trying to get in, someone else is cured."

I was angry and it showed. I'd had enough of talk.
"Get up," He told me quietly. "Pick up your mat and walk."

I stared at Him with open mouth. I did not understand.
"Get up!" He said to me again, as He held out His hand.

Strength began to flow through me, like a healing stream,
Was this Man the stirring angel, or was I living in a dream?

I made an awkward struggle, and rose from where I lay.
I knew that I must thank Him, but He had gone away.

I started out to follow Him, but I stood on tender feet,
And wobbly legs that refused to take me to the street.

I felt so strange standing there, my dearest dream was real,
My limbs belonged to me again! Now I could touch and feel!

I began to walk and with each step, I felt my strength increase,
I rolled my mat and carried it, and this I did with ease!

I was walking to my sister's house, down a narrow street,
When I was stopped and questioned by a highborn Pharisee.

"This is the Sabbath," he proclaimed. "Is that a mat you bear?
The law forbids this kind of work. I wonder that you dare!"

I looked at him and tried to think what he might want from me?
I told him that I'd just been cured; from my illness I was free!

An hour ago by the healing pool, I lay helpless and alone,
Till a stranger came and bid me rise, and take my pallet home,

'Get up,' he said, 'pick up your mat. You are healed today.'
So I arose and took my mat. There is no more to say."

"Who was the Man who bid you, to break the law and go?"
"This Man has cured me as I said. His name I do not know."

There was nothing more to tell. I left him standing there.
If he had more questions, I really didn't care.

I went home to my sister's house. She broke down in tears.
I felt like I was twelve again, and had cast off forty years.

I went to temple with my sister, later in the day.
'God had made you well', she said, 'now we ought to pray'.

I left her in the women's court, while I spent some time in thought.
I didn't understand it all, but healing had to come from God.

And then I turned and saw the Man, who had made me whole.
His eyes were piercing and I knew He looked into my soul.

"Your sins have been forgiven," He said, and held my eyes.
"Cease from sin, or worse may come. Repent now, and be wise."

He didn't have to tell me what my sins had been.
I could list them every one. I had wallowed in my sin.

I had not ever loved my God, nor loved my fellow man,
I put myself above them all, and I had made my stand.

I hated all the people, that were healed instead of me,
I lived in anger at the world, and disliked my family.

Now, I cast away my anger; and looked clearly at this Man,
I had no doubt He was the Christ, sent by the great I AM.

Peace and love came to my heart, and flooded through my soul,
Now I must go and tell the world, how Jesus made me whole!

"I know you, Lord," I said to Him. "Now, I will follow You."
"I know that God has healed me, and I've been born anew."

He smiled at me, then He was gone, my soul had been laid bare.
The time had come to thank my sister, for her years of loving care.

I know how hard it must have been, as she met my every need,
But I had shown no thankfulness, for her gentle words and deeds.

My sister loved and cared for me, just like my mother had before,
She believed I would be healed, and God's blessings were in store.

I went back to find my sister, as tears ran down my cheeks.
I wanted to say 'thank you', but I found I couldn't speak.

I stood there and held her hands, and tried to say the words,
She must know what I was feeling, and how I met the Lord.

She smiled at me and hugged me; her face was all aglow,
"Jesus," I said, and she nodded. It was all she had to know.

My world is filled with sunshine now, despite the fall of night.
Whether here or by the healing pool, my soul is filled with light.

He slowly turned to each man there with eyes that saw their worst,
"Let anyone who has no sin, come cast his stone out first."

So when they continued asking him, he lifted up himself, and said unto
them, He that is without sin among you, let him first cast a stone at her.

John 8:7 KJV

SIN NO MORE

I'd been married for ten years, and I just turned twenty-five.
We had no children, and Matthias, hardly knew I was alive.

That God had not sent us a child, seemed only common sense,
To beg my husband for a babe, could only bring offense.

I never blamed Matthias, what blame was there to see?
And yet I had the feeling, that he was blaming me.

I often prayed I'd have a babe; I could only wait and hope,
If God had other plans for us, then I must not cry and mope.

Time went by and every day, he seemed to love me less,
His indifference brought me tears, and that I must confess.

I thought he might be looking to find another wife,
Some young and pretty woman, who would brighten up his life.

I wondered if this happened, what would become of me?
Would he keep me in his house, or would he set me free?

One day in the market, I glimpsed a man I used to know;
He was the son of Father's friend, at least I thought him so.

He saw that I had noticed him, and he began to smile.
He didn't say a word to me, but watched me for a while.

I went back home with a glow, warming me inside,
To this man I was pretty; I had a creeping sense of pride.

I thought a lot about this man, though it may have been a sin.
But I was sure that I would never see this man again.

In a week while at the market, I turned and saw his face,
He was eating ripened fruit, and it was clear he liked the taste.

I knew that I should walk away; somehow this wasn't right.
But it was he who slowly turned and vanished out of sight.

I tried to please Matthias, but he seemed preoccupied,
He told me not to bother him, and I wished I hadn't tried.

Matthias was older by ten years, perhaps he saw me as a child,
Maybe there was someone else, and by her he'd been beguiled.

I thought that I must talk to him, ask him what was wrong,
Then it seemed it was my job, to stay silent and be strong.

So when I saw that man again, I returned his smile.
What could it hurt if we talked, for just a little while?

Soon, I saw him every day; for that alone I'd leave the house.
I told myself he was a friend; that I was faithful to my spouse.

We talked and laughed together, and always shared some fruit.
I thought that he was helping me, and that this was the truth.

The next day when he held my eyes, and gently took my hand,
We went together down the street, though this I hadn't planned.

He brought me back to my own home, and left me at the door,
I felt sad when he had gone, and I knew I'd wanted more.

I found him later as agreed; he saw I'd come and smiled,
And when he took my hand again, I followed like a child.

He didn't take me home this time, but down another street,
I liked the time I spent with him, and our walk was long and sweet.

Then he stopped at a stranger's house, and opened up the door,
He took my arm and drew me in, more firmly than before.

And when we stood together in a room both closed and dark,
He held me in a heavy grip, and his fingers left their mark.

His face no longer smiling, his hands too rough and strong,
I tried to pull away from him; I dared not stay there long.

He pressed me hard against the wall, then threw me on the floor,
Then he forced himself on me, till a man came through the door.

A stranger came into the room, and they yanked me to my feet,
They pulled away my clothing, and they would not let me leave.

I tried to scream, but this new man slapped his hand across my face,
I stood there nearly naked, in their shameful secret place.

And then my "friend" took silver coins, left, and went away,
This brutal man I didn't know, told me that I must stay.

He locked me in a little room with bound up hands and feet.
I knew no one could find me here, and I began to weep.

I shivered and I wept alone, all through the endless night,
When Matthias heard of this, he wouldn't want me in his sight!

At last the room grew brighter; and I had survived the night,
I still could see no way at all, out of my fearful plight.

The brutal man came again, and dragged me to the street,
I tried to pull away from him, but I only found defeat.

He was joined by several men, older and well dressed,
They didn't seem to notice I was naked and oppressed.

My clothing gone, I was ashamed, and kept my head held down,
It was early and I thanked God, few people were around.

Then with a shock I realized, where they were taking me,
We were walking toward the Teacher, who came from Galilee.

There, a group of Pharisees were standing to one side,
With smug smiles for my captors, and faces full of pride.

They led me quickly up to him, I turned my face away,
"We've caught her in adultery! What do you have you to say?"

"She was caught in the very act! She is not a faithful wife!
What would you have us do with her. The law demands her life!"

By Moses' law she must be stoned. Do you not keep the law?
The teacher knelt down in the dust, as though he never saw.

They kept on asking Him to judge, and I was full of fear.
He was writing in the dust, and he didn't seem to hear.

Again they asked this question, and their hands were full of stones,
I would have to face a judgment, before the rocks were thrown.

Now the Teacher slowly rose; He looked them in their eyes,
Still, He spoke no words to them, much to my surprise.

He slowly turned to each man there, with eyes that saw their worst,
"Let anyone who has no sin, come cast his stone out first."

The Teacher knelt in the dust again, and once more began to write,
I could not read, but those who did, took on a look of fright.

The man who was holding me, quickly took his hands away,
The Master knew what they had done, and so they dared not stay.

One by one each man left, striding quickly out of sight,
And I was left alone with Him, to make my own sins right.

He stood up and looked at me, seeing all my shame and sin,
"Have you no accusers here? Is there no one to condemn?"

"No one condemns me now, Sir. I stand here all alone."
"Nor do I condemn you, Woman. It's time that you go home."

"Go," he said, "and sin no more. Be a faithful wife."
"I do hope, Sir," I said to Him. "that such will be my life."

He smiled at me, and I felt peace settle in my soul.
Whatever happened next to me, I had been made whole.

I saw Matthias coming, as I was clutching my torn clothes,
He gently wrapped a cloak around, from my hair down to my toes.

"Wife," he said quite slowly. "You were gone all night.
Whatever happened to you, my dear, we must set it right."

"I know that I have turned from you, in anger and despair,
We had no child, and it seemed to me, that you didn't even care.

I thought I saw you had no need, or desire to be a mother.
I thought I could send you away, then I could wed another.

And yet last night when you were gone, I knew I loved you still,
I pray that you'll come back to me; please, tell me that you will."

"Matthias, I have sinned," I said. "I've been with another man.
I ask God and I ask you, to forgive me if you can."

"Someone told me," Matthias said, "where I'd find my wife",
I hurried out to fetch you. I had to somehow save your life."

"The Pharisees had set a trap for this Man from Galilee,
You were just a sacrifice, and they hurt both you and me."

"Matthias, He could see their sins, He saw my own as well.
He knew everything they'd done; they feared that He would tell."

"They walked away and I was there, to face my sin alone,
His gave me God's forgiveness; to you I must atone."

"I forgive you, Wife," he said, "though you've hurt my foolish pride,
Forgive me, please, for hurting you. I need you always by my side."

"I've prayed," I told him, "for a child, through all our married years.
I did not want to trouble you, nor burden you with my tears.

Let us pray together now, and let God see our love,
And ask Him to send us children--His blessings from above."

We walked home together then, and opened our front door,
"Welcome back, dear Wife," he said. "Let us sin no more."

My head and face were covered up with heavy linen cloth.
I tried with awkward bandaged hands, but I couldn't get it off.

*And he that was dead came forth, bound hand and foot with grave-
clothes: and his face was bound about with a napkin. Jesus saith unto
them, Loose him, and let him go.*

John 11:44 KJV

LAZARUS

This all began two years ago, and it's hard to understand,
Why I held back, and how this all, was part of Jesus' plan.

I saw Him in Jerusalem, and a crowd was gathered round,
I clearly heard every word, for no one made not a sound.

I sat down and listened, and I wondered what He meant,
His words were new and strange to me. What was His intent?

I asked Him if He'd visit us. I hoped He would be our guest.
He agreed to come and teach us, and stay a while to rest.

He brought His friends along with Him, and we were glad they came.
My sisters love excitement, and they'd heard about His fame.

We all sat and listened, my sister, Mary, at His feet.
Except for busy Martha, who would not take a seat!

I loved the stories that He told, and yet I wished I knew,
How His words applied to me, and what I ought to do.

He spoke about a rich young man, who came to Him to find,
How he could have eternal life, and ease his heart and mind.

Jesus asked this young man, what the law required of him?
The man explained he knew the law, and was careful not to sin.

He'd kept the law's commandments since he was a boy,
What was it he was lacking? Why did he have no joy?

The Master told him he required only one thing more,
He should sell what he owned, and give the money to the poor.

"When this is done, walk away, then come and follow Me."
The young man turned and left Him, and this was not to be.

He loved his money very much, and his pleasant easy life.
To think of giving this away, brought too much inner strife.

I didn't know who this man was, but the lesson I could see.
Was this something I should do? A story meant for me?

Jesus stayed with us two days, and then He left our home,
I missed Him and His teaching, and I now felt quite alone.

I looked closely at my life, and yes, I searched my very soul.
Could I leave my own dear home? Were worldly things my goal?

I thought about my sisters. They needed me right here.
If I left them on their own, I would live in guilt and fear.

And yet He said to follow Him! How could I do this thing?
His words tore me in pieces, while I was still listening.

He always stopped to visit us, whenever He passed near,
I weighed each word He uttered, and still it wasn't clear.

Yet I felt that from my life, he expected something more,
A thing beyond what I could do--leave home and close the door.

When I came home one afternoon, I felt very tired and ill.
I fell asleep and when I woke, I burned with fever still.

I downed Martha's healing draught, while she hovered by my bed.
My sister, Mary, sat by me, with a cool cloth on my head.

I took a lot of comfort that my sisters stayed close by,
It gave my heart a painful twinge, when Mary began to cry.

And then I think I slept again, for I knew no more that night.
If anything, I felt worse, when I woke to morning's light.

Martha nursed me all day long, forcing liquid through my lips,
I heard Mary's constant prayers, and I felt her fingertips.

Then before my weary eyes, the world faded and was gone.
I had no time to wonder, how my sisters would go on.

They told me later that I died--I really was quite dead.
I lay four days in the tomb--this was what they said!

I awoke in total darkness and I clearly heard His voice,
Calling me to come to Him. I knew I had made my choice.

I struggled to sit upright, on a bed that felt like stone,
Head to foot I was wrapped and bound, and totally alone.

I got slowly to my feet, though my legs would hardly bend,
I couldn't see, I couldn't breathe! This nightmare had to end!

Carefully, I tried to walk, toward a sound like grating rock,
Somewhere I heard voices, and a lot of noisy talk.

My head and face were covered up with heavy linen cloth.
I tried with awkward bandaged hands, but I couldn't get it off.

Then someone came to guide me, and then they freed my face,
I was standing on a little hill and I saw Jesus at the base.

"Help him back to his house," I heard my dear Lord say,
I leaned on Him and Martha, and Mary led the way.

He had brought me from my tomb, awakened me from death.
I consumed a hearty noonday meal, as soon I had dressed.

All our dearest friends were there; they had come to mourn,
Now they went away rejoicing, that I had been reborn.

And so we planned a dinner, a celebration meal,
Thanking God I was alive, to think and see and feel.

Jesus had accepted. He would be the honored Guest,
Many friends knew Jesus, now He would meet the rest.

Martha cooked and served the meal, everyone was there,
Mary used her precious Nard, to anoint His feet and hair.

And when the meal was finished, and we three were alone,
Mary wondered how it had been, lying on that stone.

"Lazarus," she said softly. "Was your slumber deep?
Were there dreams or visions, or just a heavy sleep?"

"To tell you both the truth" I said, "I don't remember much.
I just recall feeling ill, and my sisters' gentle touch."

In my mind were pictures, things I did not speak about.
Things that still were fuzzy, and I had to sort them out.

LAZARUS

I lay all night just thinking, until the morning light,
I went to talk with Jesus so I could set this matter right.

"Lord," I said at last to Him. "Lord, I must follow You.
I know that I'm the least of all, but it's what I have to do."

"I weep that I resisted you--this I'm sure you know!
I love you, Lord, with my whole heart, and now I long to go."

He smiled at this, and I could see the pleasure in His eyes.
My stumbling block had always been my easy pleasant life!

"My body lay there in the tomb, Lord, for four long days,
My soul was taken somewhere else, to quite another place!"

"I was in a rainbow world, beside a living stream!
I do not know if I was there, or if it was all a dream."

"When I awoke I heard Your voice, calling out to me,
"You, my Lord, of all the world. It was You I had to see!"

"I know I have to follow You. I'll leave everything behind.
God holds my sisters future, and God has eased my mind."

"Jerusalem," said Jesus, "is where I'll go to eat the feast."
"Lord," I begged, "Let me come too, though I am last and least."

"No," He told me sadly. "What is written must be done.
I will suffer at their hands, and have the help of none."

"You must remain in Bethany. It's much safer for you here.
They've made plans to seize me. And you, too, if you're near."

I thought that I had missed my chance, that it was now too late.
He refused to let me join with them. I could only pray and wait.

He departed for Jerusalem. Some disciples waited there.
Peter and John arranged the feast, which they all would share.

When He rode into the city; they welcomed Him with cheers,
It hurt me that I had no part; that He had left me here!

In days, we heard that Our dear Lord, was tortured and was tried,
And then the much more awful news, that He was crucified.

Mary knew and Martha knew, we knew and we could tell,
Just as sure as I still lived, He could arise as well.

76

And when He rose on that third day, and joy had filled my heart,
I told my sisters I was going. I was sad but we must part!

I would go and follow Him, wherever He might lead.
I will die again for Him if that is what He needs,

Mary smiled at me and wondered, why I hadn't gone before?
Martha said that they would come! Jesus always needed more!

When it was time, our Lord was gone. We watched as He ascended,
Still He promised He would be with us, until this world has ended.

It was not too late to follow Him, not while I breathed and lived!
I will do what must be done, and give all I have to give!

I pushed my way into the crowd, I must get up close and see,
I thought I recognized the Man, whose power had healed me.

And there followed him a great company of people, and of women,
which also bewailed and lamented him.

Luke 23:27 KJV

VERONICA'S VEIL

Twelve years I suffered every day. Twelve long years I waited.
The painful things that happened then, I have already stated.

I touched His hem and I am well; I live a happy life,
Helping in my brother's home, with my brother's wife.

We've journeyed to Jerusalem, where we'll eat the Feast and pray!
We came to see our sister and she insisted we must stay.

We loved shopping at the market place, so we all arose at dawn,
We broke our fast and made our list; we were eager to be gone!

The women of the household, with our baskets in our hands,
Went to purchase foodstuff, for the evening meal's demands.

It was a joy for me to be, in the company of friends,
Jesus made this happen. He brought my illness to an end.

We walked together quickly; I enjoyed the morning sun,
That warmed my chilly body, till our purchasing was done.

I wore a veil of linen, for I always felt the cold,
Twelve long years of illness had made my body old.

The day grew quickly warmer as we walked among the shops.
We chose our figs and dates and herbs, till it was time to stop.

My linen veil lay heavy now; it had become too warm,
So I tucked it in the basket that I carried on my arm.

My brother's wife smiled at me as she quickly wiped her brow,
"It's time to cook the feast," she said. "We'd better turn back now."

We turned around and started home, stopping here and there,
To look at pretty fabrics and rich coverings for our hair.

Life had now become for me, so very sweet and full,
A life renewed by Jesus, was anything but dull.

I sang His praises everywhere, I could not help but speak,
I told everyone I met, that it was Jesus they must seek.

In our path we saw a crowd, had begun to form and grow.
We could hear their noisy shouts, but their progress was quite slow.

We knew that to reach our home, we'd have to pass them by,
We hung back a little while; then thought we'd better try.

When we drew close, we realized what it was all about.
Roman soldiers had control of an angry milling crowd.

We tried to walk around the crowd, and not be in their way.
But the street was very narrow, and we could not delay.

Then I saw their prisoners; they were bearing heavy beams,
Pushed on by the Romans, harassed with jeers and screams.

One Man was just an open wound, and blood ran down His face,
He had fallen on the roadway, for He could not keep the pace.

The situation now was clear! They were carrying their own cross.
Soon they would be crucified; any hope they had was lost.

I wondered what these men had done. I wondered who they were.
Did they deserve to die this way? Whose anger had they stirred?

The fallen Man now struggled up, and tried to lift the beam.
I thought that I should go on home, and leave this awful scene.

My brother's wife tugged at my hand, urging me to come,
And still I stood there staring, and I was struck quite dumb.

I pushed my way into the crowd, I must get up close and see,
I thought I recognized the Man, whose power had healed me.

I got as close as I could get, struggling through this human tide,
Till I recognized my Savior, and I walked along beside!

He never turned to look at me; His bloody eyes were blind,
And yet He knew that I was there; this knowledge filled my mind.

How had this happened to my Lord? How had this come to be?
This Man was filled with goodness! Surely, they could see!

Jesus had healed the sick and lame and made the dead arise!
Jairus' daughter lives today! She was healed before their eyes!

They must not do this awful thing; I loudly shouted, "No!"
"He is our Savior and our Lord! You have to let Him go!"

No one even looked at me. No one heard my cry.
Shouting covered up my voice, but I wouldn't be passed by.

Then I watched as He was pushed by a Roman guard,
He stumbled on a dislodged stone, and then He went down hard.

It was clear to all He could not rise, could no longer lift the cross,
The guards were looking all around, for someone to accost.

I pushed through and ran to Him, and knelt there by His side,
My linen veil was in my hands, so I could clean his face and eyes.

I gently wiped the blood away, so He could see once more,
Perhaps, I could help to ease, this heavy load He bore.

He placed His hand over mine, and pressed the fabric to His face,
I recalled for just an instant that other time and place.

"Please, my Lord," I whispered. "They cannot do this to you!"
"What is written, must be done. The prophet's words are true."

His voice was hoarse and gasping. His words were full of pain.
Then He took His hand away, and tried to rise again.

Someone came, gave Him a hand, and helped lift up the beam;
Jesus struggled to His feet, in this pain-filled nightmare dream.

I followed as closely as I could, till the crowd pushed me away,
Then I walked behind them, and with a weeping heart I prayed.

My brother's wife now joined with me, her arm was linked with mine.
She understood now Who this was, and that we must take the time.

The other women went back home, but we followed all the way,
The others could go and leave us here, but we would have to stay.

We walked behind them to the hill, afraid of what we'd see,
Still not comprehending how such an awful thing could be.

We watched them drive the iron nails through His hands and feet,
The sun beat down on everyone, with nauseating heat.

Then we watched them raise the cross, through a blur of tears,
There were two women close to Him, their faces white with fear.

I heard Him speak forgiveness to those who caused His pain,
I heard every word He spoke, as His life began to wane.

Then He was gone and the bright hot day, became as dark as night.
I knew this darkness had to come, because He was the Light.

I felt the ground begin to shake, and fear gripped us every one.
A soldier whispered what I knew, "This surely was God's Son".

We turned away to slowly walk back to our sister's home,
Though we were still together, we were terribly alone.

Then my brother came to meet us, and share our homeward walk,
To keep us safe in this early dark, and listen to our talk.

We told him what had happened, and what befell our Lord,
We recounted every detail, and repeated every word.

Passover was upon us but we did not eat the feast.
Every joy had left us, down to the very least.

All I felt was great despair, I could not even cry,
I had no desire at all to sleep so I didn't even try.

Next morning my dear brother's wife came and sat by me,
"The veil you used to clean His face--will you let me see?"

I saw again His bleeding face and felt His gentle touch,
I had tried to wipe the blood away, but there had been so much...

I went and found that crumpled veil, made of linen soft and old,
Blood that streamed from His wounded face, stained every crease and fold.

I held it gently for I knew, this blood was from my Lord,
What I saw when I spread it out was piercing as a sword.

His wounded face was imprinted there, and any eye could see,
The mirror of His countenance entrusted now--to me!

My brother and his loving wife, gazed and so did I,
At the priceless gift He'd given, as He went to die.

COME, FOLLOW ME

My Savior died there on the cross, while the world just looked aside,
But in three days, He rose again, and all our tears were dried.

I've met His friends and followers; I've joined them in "The Way".
To love my Lord and do His will, shall fill my every day.

83

"Carry it!" I heard the shout, and felt a heavy striking blow,
They laid the wooden beam on me, though why I didn't know.

*And they compel one Simon a Cyrenian, who passed by, coming out of
the country, the father of Alexander and Rufus, to bear his cross.*

Mark 15:21 KJV

SIMON OF CYRENE

We'd come near a thousand miles, walking mostly all the way,
My plans were good; we had arrived, for a Jew's most sacred day!

That God would guide us safely here, had been my fervent prayer.
So when I saw the temple mount, I could only stand and stare.

I gazed out at Jerusalem--the city of my soul,
I'd dreamed of David's city, to see it was my goal!

Passover in Jerusalem! With Jews from everywhere,
Gathered here to worship the one true God we share.

My brother came to visit here, several years ago,
He stayed and had a family, that I do not even know.

My children were still sleeping at a country inn nearby,
So I walked into the city, to feast my eager eyes.

I thought I should have brought my wife, she must see this too!
Gazing at Jerusalem made my weary life seem new.

I hurried toward this city! I longed to walk those streets.
I was thirsting then to drink it in, to taste and find it sweet!

I knew that there were Romans here. I knew they ruled the land.
But I also knew that God had charge, and we all were in His hand.

I was drawing ever closer, to the place I longed to be,
While a crowd of noisy people were coming out toward me.

They were soldiers from the look of them, with loud and angry voices.
They had an ugly job to do, but soldiers have few choices.

I saw that they had prisoners, and a crowd had gathered round.
I heard both jeers and weeping, and it was a painful sound.

Three men hefted wooden beams, on shoulders raw and bare,
One was marked by savage beating, but these people didn't care.

He stumbled and recovered, and with trembling knees He stood,
Till He got a better grip, on the heavy blood soaked wood.

One soldier tried to speed Him up, and pushed Him from behind,
So then He tripped and stumbled; His blood filled eyes were blind.

The other two walked ahead, carrying their own beam,
They were in a living nightmare, however it might seem!

I couldn't turn my eyes away, from this wounded bleeding Man,
I stood and stared like all the rest, and forgot my careful plan.

I tried to move out of their way, so the mob could pass me by,
But they just carried me along, toward the place these men would die.

I knew what the beams were for; they would help to form a cross,
A criminal would be nailed there, until his life was lost.

These men were all convicted of breaking Roman law,
But the object of the cruel jeers; who was this man I saw?

There were women in the crowd; and I watched them shedding tears,
I could see they truly loved this Man, and I could see their awful fears.

What had He done to earn their love, and to draw the others hate?
What had He done to bring about this deadly awful fate?

I stared in fascination; He looked up and met my eyes,
Overwhelming pain was there, and a peace I can't deny.

Soon He stumbled yet again; I watched helpless as He fell.
I heard a woman's choking scream; from where I could not tell.

I felt an open-handed blow, and it pushed me toward the beam.
"Pick it up and carry it!" I was in their dreadful dream!

I walked over to the fallen One, and there put out my hand.
In my grip He rose again, and swayed till He could stand.

"Carry it!" I heard the shout, and felt a heavy striking blow,
They laid the wooden beam on me, though why I didn't know.

Fear and anger filled my soul; they put His cross on me!
What I had to do with Him, was nothing I could see.

I turned my head to see His face; as we labored side by side.
He was ready now to take His cross, He came to me and tried.

He shoved His bleeding shoulder beneath my heavy load,
I felt the burden lessen, as we slowly walked that road.

Again I looked into His eyes; and saw His perfect peace,
I felt the love come out of Him, and I felt my anger cease.

"Who are you?" I gasped out to Him, expecting no reply.
"Why have they done this thing to you? Can you tell me why?"

His breath was choked and labored; Was He to die right here?
He formed the words, "Just forgive." The effort cost Him dear.

I bore the crossbeam's weight for Him; what I did was good,
I had to help this dying Man, in any way I could.

They kept us both together, in that cruel Roman yoke,
My skin was torn and bleeding, and neither of us spoke.

Our journey finally ended, there on a sloping hill,
My time of pain was over, but His worst was waiting still.

I told myself to go away and not watch what they would do,
His head was bowed, accepting, unlike the other two.

Still, I stood there staring, tears and sweat ran down my face,
While He was mocked and brutalized in that killing place.

A woman stood across from me, with horror in her eyes,
I watched her bite into her lips, to stifle her own cries.

When they nailed His feet and hands, and when they raised the cross,
Blood streamed from her wounded lips, her silence had a cost.

Her face went white, and then I saw she was slipping to the ground,
A young man caught her in his arms; she hadn't made a sound.

On the cross and looking down, His eyes were seeking hers.
I thought He whispered, "Mother," but I wasn't really sure.

He looked at those who tortured him, and His grief was raw and new.
"Father, please forgive them, for they don't know what they do."

The taunts and jests of passers-by made this scene more grim.
To forget their gnawing guilt, they were mocking Him.

The soldiers now stayed busy, not looking at the crosses;
They gambled for His garments, complaining of their losses.

One soldier nailed a sign above His bowed and bleeding head,
"King of the Jews" in three tongues, was what it clearly said.

'King of the Jews,' I asked myself, what this sign might mean!
There was Pilate and Herod and Caesar, but no real Jewish king.

Now He caught the woman's eye and begged her to come near,
Supported by the young man's arm, she came close to hear.

"Woman," He gasped with halting breath, "This man is now your son."
"Now this woman is your mother; please do this for me, John."

He had finished His last instruction. He let His head fall down,
"It is finished," I heard Him gasping. "Father, take my spirit now."

I heard His final dying cry, and the ground beneath was shaking,
I wondered as the sky grew dark, was I asleep or waking?

Soldiers came and broke the legs of the other men,
They thrust a sword into His side. and drew it out again.

He made no sound for life had gone, but the weeping woman screamed.
The man named John stayed with her--he was now her son, it seemed.

A soldier looking up at Him, spoke the words that filled my heart.
"This surely was the Son of God." From this thought I can't depart."

The world lay now in darkness though the time was afternoon,
I thought my soul was torn to bits; my heart an open wound.

A young woman came and stood by me, as I turned to walk away.
"Thank you, Sir, for helping Him," was what I heard her say.

"Who is He then?" I asked her, as I turned to meet her eyes.
"He is Jesus, God's own son, and that's why He had to die."

"I really do not understand, but He told us this would come.
I know I still believe in Him, though my soul has gone quite numb."

She looked sadly at the place where His mother leaned on John,
She said she thought though He was dead, He somehow wasn't gone.

"Who are you, Woman?" I inquired. "You are all so very brave."
"I'm Mary Magdalene," she said, "And now we'll follow to His grave."

She hurried to the other two, and they mourned together there.
It was time to seek the temple, time to find a place for prayer.

I found everyone was talking, when I reached the temple ground,
How the holy curtain ripped apart, with an awful tearing sound.

Only a priest could pass that curtain, where God was known to be,
Now God, Himself, has ripped it down, or so it seemed to me.

Full of sorrow and confusion, I went to find my wife.
The wonder of this city blurred, as I wept for His lost life.

I tried to tell my brother about this suffering Man,
But my words came out so broken, he couldn't understand.

I later found the others, those who followed Him,
I learned then He could forgive, my each and every sin.

His friends all thought that He was gone, and that included me,
But in three days He arose, for all of us to see.

Looking back, I thought that day was the worst I'd ever lived.
Now I see that painful day was God's most precious gift.

"Today," He gasped, "You'll come and be, with Me in Paradise."
His head dropped down upon His chest, then He closed His eyes.

*42 And he said unto Jesus, Lord, remember me when thou comest into
thy kingdom.*
*43 And Jesus said unto him, Verily I say unto thee, Today shalt thou be
with me in paradise.*

Luke 23:42,43

HEAVEN THIS AFTERNOON

Susannah is my sister; and she also is my twin.
She is always there to finish, any story I begin.

Susannah was sixteen when she married my best friend,
Not one of us could foresee, how all this would end.

 Soon there was a newborn girl, and then a baby boy,
They lived on very little, but they gave each other joy.

Daniel and Susannah were faithful in their prayers,
I turned my face away from God. For me, He wasn't there.

A potter hired Daniel; he came to love the potter's clay,
As he improved, his hard work, would bring him better pay.

It was for their children sake, that I first began to steal.
They were poor and the children's needs, were hard and very real.

I wanted them to have the things more money would allow,
So I brought them food and drink, and their lives were better now.

My sister's life was easier, with the gifts I often gave,
She had a little extra, and that little she could save.

I was angry that the Romans, had occupied our land.
It was wrong that wealth and power, came quickly to their hand.

I knew of one such wealthy man. I watched him every day,
A centurion called Marius, and it was fitting that he pay.

Once I made delivery on a load of fruit and bread,
For a banquet he was hosting; or so his servant said.

I often make deliveries to homes of wealthy men,
Sometimes they don't count the goods, when I bring them in.

I held back a thing or two, some bread and figs and dates.
I smiled to think about his food, on our supper plates.

It's true I took things when I could, I stole from many men,
I planned someday (except for Romans) to give it back again.

These Romans were invaders; my anger became hate,
I aimed it all at Marius, and his unearned estate.

One day my sister was at market, shopping for the feast,
I was helping with her baskets, as her load increased.

Passover is a special time and she took her savings with her,
I knew she had a good meal planned, and I loved my special sister.

She seemed so bright and happy, as she decided what to buy,
Then I caught a glimpse of Marius, from the corner of my eye.

He watched us closely as we walked through the market place,
I wondered if he watched Susannah, or did he know my face?

When we turned to walk back home, about the middle of the day,
Marius was watching still, and stepped up to bar the way.

"I thought I recognized you. You deliver food and wine."
His voice was pleasant, but his eyes, looked directly into mine.

"You have a pretty wife," he said. "And have you children too?"
"Susannah is my sister, Sir, and we have errands we must do."

This centurion stared long at me, with a warning I could read,
Then he looked hard at my sister, and his finger touched her cheek.

Susannah jerked away from him, and I pulled her to my side,
Then we quickly walked away, and I saw her face was white.

I hated Marius before, now my feelings reached a boil,
All I had taken from his house, was bread and fruit and oil.

But he had touched my sister! These Romans were a blight!
I burned to do something now, to set this matter right.

I quickly walked Susannah home, where I told her she must stay,
A plan was forming in my mind; I would deal with him today.

I walked to his home a different way; I stayed close by to wait,
When he came home at dinner time, he would meet his fate!

I hid there in the shadows and watched the darkness fall.
Then I climbed into a tree, and dropped down beyond his wall.

I picked a place where I could see him, coming through the gate,
Soon this Roman soldier, would taste my anger and my hate!

It wasn't long till he returned, he entered and passed near.
He was whistling as he walked, I could see he felt no fear.

Rage was filling up my soul, I gripped the dagger in my hand.
I would make an end of him, and leave him lifeless in the sand.

I felt ready to make my move! Now, I must strike him down,
But Marius kept walking, and he never looked around.

I was burning as he passed me by, but I wasn't any threat,
My anger turned against myself. I swore I'd get him yet!

Something deep within me wouldn't let me take his life.
Still there were things that I could do, to cut him down to size!

In a while the lamps went out, the household was asleep.
All was total silence. And I'd made a promise I must keep.

I entered through a window, into the dark and gloom,
I knew the place he kept his coins; I went directly to that room.

My luck still held and I lifted up, the corner of the rug,
The bag was nestled in the wall, securely as a bug.

I drew it out and couldn't help, the smile that crossed my face.
I crept back toward the window, so I could leave this place.

With no warning I found myself, face down on the floor,
Someone's foot was on my back, and someone blocked the door.

I had fallen in his baited trap, that I'd been too blind to see.
This Roman had me in his grip. How much did he hate me?

They dragged me through his courtyard and out into the street,
Marius was smiling when he said revenge was sweet.

He smiled while I was beaten, and thrown into a cell,
There was another man there, who'd been beaten up as well.

He had a bruised and swollen face, and a laugh that brought a chill,
"Glad to meet you, Friend," he said. "Now they've got one more to kill."

I lay for hours on the floor, in a flood of throbbing pain,
Inside I flailed in black despair, then they dragged me out again.

My hands were bound behind me, and they put shackles on my feet,
I was brought before a Roman court; I just hoped they'd let me speak.

Marius accused me. He looked pleased to see me there.
Fear consumed my very soul, but I knew he didn't care.

Marius said I was a thief. That I stole his bag of gold.
The court said that I was guilty, and Roman law was cold.

I waited in a nightmare till the sentence had come down,
I thought they'd give me lashes, and drive me out of town.

"Crucify" was what they said--that was what I heard.
It hit me like a hammer, that cruel Roman word.

I wanted to see my sister, and talk to my best friend,
I tried to think of something, some message I could send!

I thought it would be tomorrow. I thought there would be time,
I thought there must be some way out, if I just used my mind.

In the street I saw the man, who shared my cell last night,
His eyes were filled with terror, and his skin was very white.

As we stood there shaking, they brought forth another Man.
He was bruised and cut and battered, till He could barely stand.

A crowd surged forth around Him, many called His name.
Some people seemed to hate Him, and were glad He was in pain.

Now that there were three of us, they brought the wooden beams,
I tried to think this was not real; but the worst of Satan's dreams.

With the crossbeam on my shoulders, I bowed beneath it's weight,
I stared at the Roman soldiers, and again I felt my hate.

I looked over at this third Man, and at His blood-streaked face,
He showed no fear that I could see, no hatred for this place.

We struggled slowly onward, down the rough and crowded road,
The Man behind was gasping now, as He tried to bear His load.

They cursed Him for His weakness, they struck Him and He fell,
While my day seemed like a nightmare, His day was utter hell.

Soon enough He fell again; and someone helped Him rise,
This man they forced to bear the cross, much to my surprise.

I knew where we were going, and it was not far away.
I dreaded every footstep and I prayed for a delay.

I still did not believe in God. I was not a praying man.
Yet my lips were moving in a prayer, and I couldn't understand.

I continued praying with each step, begging God to grant me life.
I wanted to live and grow old, with children and a wife.

When we reached the hillside, where the heavy crosses lay,
My mouth was dry, my knees were weak, cold sweat ran down my face.

My cellmate was the first they chose; his screams cut through the air!
Blood flowed from his wrists and feet, and I thought he'd die right there.

Roman hands grabbed hold of me, and threw me on the cross,
My skull banged hard against the wood, as I tried to fight them off.

Nails were tearing through my flesh, I screamed and no one cared,
And when I opened up my eyes, I saw my sister there.

When my cross was upright, I could not think or see,
All I could do was beg our God that He remember me.

I never saw the third cross rise, and I think He made no sound,
My soul had melted into pain. I never looked around.

I thought that if I had to die, I prayed it would be soon.
Agony washed over me, from each and every wound.

Raucous taunts, and mocking shouts were thrown out by the crowd,
"Son of God, save Yourself," they screamed, and laughed out loud.

I heard my cellmate's bitter jeer, he was blaspheming too,
"Prove you are the Son of God, and bring us down with you!"

Now I knew this blameless Man; this Man from Galilee,
There was no stain of guilt in Him, as there was guilt in me.

I had to speak--I had to say--the words rushed to my mind!
All my life, I saw now, I had chosen to be blind.

"We are thieves, we're criminals, and we deserve to die!
This Man Jesus has not sinned--unlike you and I."

"If He is King of the Jews, and God has sent Him here,
Can you speak so to the Christ, and yet you feel no fear?"

Susannah had told me of this Man, but I had turned away,
My very soul was black with sin; there was more I had to say.

"When you come into your kingdom, Lord, please remember me!"
I felt His peace flood through my soul, as I felt Him set me free."

His voice was hoarse and shaking, and He labored just to speak.
He was giving me a miracle, when He already was too weak."

"Today," He gasped, "You'll come and be, with Me in Paradise."
His head dropped down upon His chest, then He closed His eyes.

He gave His spirit up to God, and I heard Him breathe His last,
I knew for sure I would go with Him, and I prayed it would be fast.

Women were weeping at His feet, and one stood there by me.
Susannah was smiling as she wept, knowing Jesus set me free.

"Susannah," I cried out to her, slowly, lest I choke,
"Sister, tell my story, please." she nodded as I spoke.

Then the ground began to tremble, night blotted out the day.
"This surely was the Son of God," I heard one soldier say.

The voice I heard was Marius. He was standing by my cross.
"I'll keep your family in my care. I shall make up their loss."

"I never thought that you would die. I could have stayed my hand.
God forgive me for these things I've done. I didn't understand."

I tried hard to speak to Marius. I wanted him to know,
I surely brought this on myself. You reap just what you sow.

Someone else came close to me. I glimpsed him in the dark.
There by my legs, he drew back his sword, and I knew he'd leave his mark.

I screamed aloud in molten pain; I heard the breaking bones.
I sank down and could not breathe, and my Savior took me home.

We stood together by the cross, where He suffered and He died,
When they took Him to the tomb, we walked there by His side.

*And the women also, which came with him from Galilee, followed after,
and beheld the sepulchre, and how his body was laid.*

Luke 23:55

THE FIRST DAY

I truly thought two days ago, that my life was at an end.
The shattered self I had become, not even God could mend.

The greatest Love of all my life, was torn away from me,
How I continued to draw breath, was more than I could see.

We stood together by the cross, where He suffered and He died,
When they took Him to the tomb, we walked there by His side.

He was gone, the world was dark, night was in my soul,
There was nothing on this earth, left to make me whole.

I wept there with His mother, as we left the tomb,
Then we joined the others, in an upper room.

We couldn't eat or drink, nor could we sleep or rest,
I couldn't stop remembering, though I did my best.

In my mind I saw the miles, that we had walked together,
Through the hills of Galilee, through every kind of weather.

I followed Him from Magdala, where He came and set me free,
From seven fearful demons, that were controlling me.

Those demons came and brought with them, an all-consuming fear,
When they spoke into my mind, it was all that I could hear!

My soul dissolved in panic; I lived in nightmare places,
I don't know what I said or did; I could only see their faces.

Then one day I saw Him, standing like a shaft of light,
In the center of my private hell, and His brightness filled my sight.

He cast those demons out of me, that occupied my mind,
And made me whole, and I could see, the sun begin to shine.

Of course, I followed after Him, I loved Him and His mother,
For me, and for His closest friends, we could do no other.

We watched Him as He healed the sick, and fed the multitudes!
He taught us and He prayed with us, during quiet interludes.

We thought our precious time with Him, would last for many years,
We didn't know His life would end, leaving us with tears and fears.

The common folk adored Him, and would have made Him king,
But many others feared His power, more than anything.

The money that my parents left, when they passed away,
I spent it gladly for our needs, so we had enough each day.

I remembered all these things, and my mind went round and round,
Till I was dizzy with just thinking, and peace could not be found.

I feared the demons might return for I could not control my sorrow.
I thought they'd creep inside my mind, and I'd find them there tomorrow.

When daylight came I had no tears, for I had shed them all,
I shook with weariness and cold, as I huddled by the wall.

His mother came and sat with me; I was glad to have her near.
She shared with me her suffering, and this I held most dear.

She whispered many words to me; how she always knew,
There were hard important things He was sent by God to do.

This long Sabbath brought no joy, we never left the room,
The women planned to go tomorrow, with spices to the tomb.

To anoint His broken body, was the thing we focused on,
We all agreed the spices, must be at the tomb by dawn.

The disciples warned us not to go, we were in danger still,
Did we want to give the Romans, his followers to kill?

The evening of the Sabbath, at last I fell asleep;
An exhausted, fitful slumber, anything but deep.

The room was dark when I awoke, in the upper room,
I gladly left my fearful dreams, to take spices to His tomb.

Spices to anoint His body; our one last chance to serve!
Quietly, I woke the women, to go and do what He deserved!

So quietly, we left the house, while the others lay in sleep,
It was the day we waited for; the first day of the week.

Nothing could be done on Sabbath, but rest and try to pray,
But now we could go forth again, it was a working day.

They laid Him there, and with the stone, they had closed the door,
I thought then that I would never see Him anymore.

Now I thought to say aloud, "We must roll the stone away!"
Then, "Perhaps there is a gardener, coming here today."

We longed to see our Lord again, though He lay still and cold,
We'd apply the fragrant spices, when the stone was rolled.

We searched and quickly found the tomb, though the morning was still dark,
And then we thought that we were wrong, that we had missed the mark.

The doorway now stood open, the stone was rolled away,
Why had the tomb been opened, before the light of day?

They must have moved the body, of our precious Lord,
They must have laid Him elsewhere, and given us no word.

We wondered what had happened and looked for any sign,
Then we went into the tomb, wondering what we'd find.

We saw the tomb was empty now; His body was not there,
This brought to us an added grief, that would have to bear.

We slowly walked around the cave, wondering who knew
Where they might have taken Him, and deciding what to do.

We stayed close by the empty tomb; I bent my head and wept,
I had so longed to see my Lord, if only as He slept.

We still were there beside the cave at breaking of the dawn,
Someone took our Lord away, and we must know where He'd gone

And then I saw two figures, standing in the early light,
They had bright and shining faces, their garments gleaming white.

We watched them coming closer! We felt wonderment and fear,
Were these mortal men or angels, that were drawing near?

My eyes were hurting with the light, and so I looked away,
They had kind and gentle voices, soft as the break of day.

"Why do you seek the living, here amongst the dead?
He is not here! He is risen! Remember what He said!"

He told you while in Galilee, He must be crucified.
On the dawning of the third day, then He would arise!"

"Yes," I whispered, "I remember. He told us all those things."
"Go, then, and tell the others! Let your feet have wings."

I hurried back with this news straight to the upper room,
I told them what the men had said; He was no longer in the tomb!

They stared at me in disbelief, I could see it in their eyes.
It was John who hurried to the door! He ran out with a cry.

Peter followed after him, and I ran along behind!
I thought I knew exactly what the two would find.

But morning's light showed something I hadn't seen before,
Grave clothes lying in a heap, glimpsed through the open door.

The linen cloth that bound His head, lay folded and alone,
These were the only items in that empty room of stone.

John and Peter turned away, to go and join the others,
Wondering still what it meant, and what to tell the brothers.

I stayed there beside the tomb. It was a weary watch I kept,
I hadn't seen my precious Savior, so I bent my head and wept.

"He's alive," was what they said--those men in shining white,
But Peter still seemed to doubt! Could it be that Peter's right?

I looked up and there I saw, a workman standing near.
This must be a gardener! And I watched him without fear.

"Woman, who are you looking for? Why is it that you weep?"
He spoke to me so gently, but his concern seemed real and deep.

"Please, Sir," I said humbly, "I am searching for my Lord,
Do you know where He's been moved? Have you any word?"

"This tomb, I know, was given Him, by a wealthy man,
It wasn't His! If He's been moved, please tell me if you can."

"I will go and fetch Him, and bring Him to the others!
We want to anoint His body--His disciples and His mother."

"Mary," He said softly, and I knew that gentle tone,
"Mary," He repeated, and I stumbled back against the stone.

That was the voice of Jesus! He turned and I could see,
My Savior standing there alive, looking straight at me.

"Teacher!" I cried, with tears of joy, and I fell down at His feet,
Where I saw the nail wounds, and my belief was made complete.

He was smiling as He said, "You must leave me here and go,
Tell my disciples I am risen, You've seen me, and you know."

"Tell them I go to Galilee, as I said to them before,
Tell them we'll be together, by the sea once more!"

Reluctantly, I turned from Him. It was clear I could not stay,
And when I turned to look again, He had gone away.

When I told the others, that I saw Him there alive,
Some of them doubted still, and would only believe their eyes.

I knew that He would come to them, just as He came to me,
I knew He'd always be there, if they had faith enough to see.

Days ago my life seemed over; all good was at an end,
But now I have the boundless joy, that only God can send.

This is the day our Lord has made, the first day of the week,
The day of resurrection, and life for all who seek!

ABOUT THE COVER ARTIST

Through her artwork, Karen wishes to convey the connection she
believes we all have with the spiritual and unseen reality around us.
A devout Catholic, Karen would like to share her faith and love of God
through her art.

Karen chooses watercolor as her medium because of its translucent
qualities which enhance a sense of light. She prefers using a vivid color
palette, representing the brightness and beauty of creation and of heaven.
Her work consists mainly of Christian images, angels, flowers, landscapes
and lighthouses. Knowing of the importance of our homes,
Karen also paints House Portraits on commission.

Karen hopes that her artwork will stir the soul, planting little seeds of
faith in those who view it, drawing them closer to Christ through the
workings of the Holy Spirit.

Karen resides in Stevensville, Michigan, with her husband Greg,
daughters Gina and Angela and dog Millie.

You may contact her via her studio email address:
karengaravaliaart@comcast.net

or you can find her facebook page at:
Original Watercolors by Karen Garavalia